ENDOR

"Kevin has written a book that applies to all of us! He is honest about his pain, clear about how we all carry a wound, and hopeful as he points us to the Healer. Get this book. Read it! Share it!" Dean Fulks- Lead Pastor, Lifepoint Church

"Kevin is a longtime friend of mine who has experienced life's challenges that readers will quickly relate to. His situation made him question his faith but ultimately led him to grow closer to the Lord and truly live out his faith." Ryan Smith- State Representative, Ohio House District 93

"Kevin challenges our motivations for faith. Christians have been motivated by and conditioned to accept comfortable, easy, immediate, casual and rule-complying Christianity as God's blessings. Kevin provides a better, more effective motivation in this book: the integration of faith and life experiences through the pursuit of God and God alone." Sam Rosa- Senior Pastor, Delaware Christian Church

"This book is so relevant for Christians in America today. For those who are willing to hear what Kevin is saying, this is a life-changing message. More importantly, it has the power to be a Christian culture-changing message." Amber Nelson- CEO, Lantern Property LLC

"Kevin vividly describes his transformation from spiritual death to life in the milieu of the American middle class with all of its attendant distractions from true intimacy with God. I'm thankful that he was called to share this story of hope with others who may be awakened from their present spiritual sleepwalking to a fuller relationship with

Jesus Christ." Richard M. Garner- Partner, Collins Roche Utley & Garner, LLC

"Kevin's life challenges have provided him the opportunity to share his story about how Christ-Followers are being deceived by the American Dream." Ric Bishop- Partner, Engenesys

"*American Pharisee* inspires readers to search their hearts for the truth and explores the pathway to experience God's peace and restoration through suffering." Sherry Bockert- Vice President, Citigroup

"Kevin addresses the 'successful' 21st century American Christian who is suddenly rocked by an unforeseen tragic circumstance that brings him to a crossroads of faith. He asks hard-hitting questions about God, faith, and self in a manner that is personal and relevant to all Christians who seek to know God more intimately." John Cassell- Executive Director, Cornerstone Family Services

AMERICAN
PHARISEE

KEVIN HOVER

Printed in the United States of America

Scripture taken from the NEW AMERICAN STANDARD BIBLE®, Copyright © 1960, 1962, 1963, 1968, 1971, 1972, 1973, 1975, 1977, 1995 by The Lockman Foundation. Used by permission.

Published by Author Academy Elite
PO Box 43, Powell, OH 43035
www.AuthorAcademyElite.com

Paperback ISBN: 978-1-64085-811-4
Hardcover ISBN: 978-1-64085-812-1
e-book ISBN: 978-1-64085-813-8

Library of Congress Control Number: 2019910911

Available in hardcover, softcover, e-book, and audiobook

To my wife and 3 daughters
for making our journey rich and beautiful

CONTENTS

INTRODUCTION

Warning: This book is going to challenge your faith to its core. If I achieved my goal in writing this book, then it should cause you to pause and reflect on your own personal relationship with God. This might be an uncomfortable experience, but I highly encourage you to embrace the discomfort and ask God to expose anything that might be creating a barrier that prevents you from experiencing Him to the fullest. In doing so, the temporary discomfort you feel in wrestling with your faith will provide an opportunity to draw closer to God. Simply put—this could be one of the biggest steps you take in your faith journey with Christ. However, it may require you to get out of your comfort zone in order to truly pursue God with a heart fully surrendered to Him.

As Americans, we tend to treasure independence, freedom, and prosperity. Our country was founded upon independence, and generally speaking, all of mankind, regardless of the culture, admires the trait of self-sufficiency. Many Americans who claim a faith in Jesus Christ tend to follow this same philosophy and fail to realize that putting too much emphasis on these principles can actually become harmful to their relationship with Christ. Self-sufficiency is a good thing, but living the Christian life independently from God—no matter how moral, ethical, or upright a person claims to be—will ultimately draw one further away from God instead of closer to Him. These people admittedly suffer from a stale and boring faith experience. They recognize something is missing and that God feels distant. More likely than not, culture is negatively affecting their faith walk. This book will confront the common American beliefs that can negatively affect one's relationship with the Lord and provide solutions to cultivate a thriving and flourishing relationship with God.

Many who have decided to follow Christ quickly fall into what I call the American Pharisee lifestyle. An American Pharisee is one who claims Christ as Savior, yet allows the surrounding culture to negatively influence one's faith instead of using that faith to positively influence the culture. The result is often that people who believe they are legitimately following Christ actually live independently from him by pursuing something other than a growing relationship with him. Usually, the other pursuit is some form of happiness, comfort, or success. Specifically, **it is a lifestyle that attempts to use faith as a tool or mechanism to assist with achieving some other goal of happiness, comfort, or success.** In this context, the person's primary desire to worship God is motivated by receiving blessings from God instead of being connected to God. It is a "safe" form of Christianity because it doesn't require any great sacrifice or commitment that might get in the way of pursuing one's goals in life. If things aren't going well, American Pharisees believe the solution is to muster up enough self-discipline, motivation, and willpower to increase their faith so that their circumstances will turn around. And, as long as things are going well, American Pharisees will continue pursuing the good life and work in their Christian duties as long as they fit conveniently within their busy schedules. American Pharisees completely miss the point that God IS the blessing.

The American Pharisee lifestyle moves at a rapid pace focused on **attaining, achieving, and acquiring.** It is a lifestyle that tends to **establish high moral standards,** yet either ignores those standards altogether or follows them rigorously to the point of judging others who are unable to live up to those standards. It is a lifestyle where people will tend to feel pretty good about themselves most of the time, but there's also a recognition that something is missing in their faith walk.

Symptoms of being an American Pharisee include:

- Experiencing little spiritual growth or connectedness with Christ

- Pursuing personal desires over God's desires

- Focusing on life's circumstances instead of God's promises

- Consistently experiencing high levels of stress, anxiety, and worry

- Possessing a mindset that God is distant and detached from the world

- Frequently questioning or even doubting the Bible because it appears to contradict current circumstances

American Pharisees will tend to respond to these symptoms by:

- Focusing solely on God's commands and Christian disciplines (attending church, reading the Bible, praying, etc.)

- Trying harder to produce the fruit of the Spirit (love, joy, peace, patience, kindness, goodness, faithfulness, and self-control) by their own exertion

- Striving to sin less and serve God more in order to receive a blessing

- Pursuing a good and nice life over pursuing God

- Becoming consumed and overwhelmed with life's circumstances

Instead of curing these symptoms, American Pharisees actually worsen their condition because they believe the lie that hard work, dedication, motivation, and self-discipline can fix a person's spiritual condition, but that is not how God designed it.

I have been a Christ-follower for most of my life. However, I'm disappointed that for many of those years, I have lived this American Pharisee lifestyle. It's something that I'm not proud of, but I'm so thankful that God has been patient with me over the years. He has never given up on me, and He has not given up on you either.

God has created a way for us to truly experience Him here and now this very day. We no longer have to live a life where God feels distant and where life is spinning out of control. Eternal life with God begins the day we make the decision to follow Him—not merely when we get to Heaven. When we decide to follow God above all else, instead of simply considering Him as one of several options, we will become equipped with everything we need to experience true freedom. And this freedom allows us to enjoy a life that is so much fuller and more satisfying than we could ever imagine. Eternal life is to know God and Jesus Christ whom He sent (John 17:3). It's a journey that will last throughout eternity because we will never be able to fully comprehend the infinite greatness and majesty of God.

If you've made the decision to follow Christ at some point in your life but feel stuck in your spiritual journey, then this book will help you identify your sticking point and provide a way to get "un-stuck." If you haven't yet made the decision to follow Christ or are unsure about what it even means to be a Christian, I highly encourage you to read this book as well. I'm confident it will expose some of the popular, modern-day myths of what it means to be a Christian and teach you Biblical truths about living a fulfilling, thriving, exciting, and—yes—even fun life that is rooted in Christ. The Christian life was never meant to be boring, dull, and lifeless. Unfortunately, mankind has done a very effective job at making the Christian lifestyle unappealing, not only for unbelievers, but for believers as well.

As long as we live in this broken world, we will be susceptible to living the American Pharisee life. None of us are exempt from it, so all of us must constantly be on guard. Therefore, as Christ-followers, we must be vigilant in making sure the American Pharisee does not live inside of us.

In this book, I will share with you real life experiences, what I learned from them, and how I've grown in my spiritual walk with Christ throughout these experiences. Along the way, I have made some poor choices and have also experienced tremendous hardships that were out of my control. I even came to the point where I was so upset with God that I was ready to give up on Him and walk away from Him altogether. But even in that very moment, God never gave up on me and saw me through the absolute lowest point in my life—even when I didn't think He was by my side. Looking back on my personal turmoil, I know without a doubt that He never left me, but rather I created barriers throughout my years of being an American Pharisee. Those barriers prevented me from experiencing a close and intimate relationship with Him. God not only saw me through those darkest moments, but He completely redeemed my brokenness and made it into something more beautiful than I could have ever have imagined. God wants to do the same thing with you. My hope is that you will identify the barriers that are preventing you from fully experiencing God and have the courage to take the steps of faith to allow those barriers to be removed.

When it comes right down to it, I am no different than you. I have experienced many highs and lows in my spiritual journey, and looking back, I can truly say that my spiritual lows were not necessarily the times when I experienced hurt, sadness, or despair. Rather, my real spiritual lows occurred at points in my life when I decided to follow the American Pharisee lifestyle instead of following Christ. I learned all of this through suffering, and now I have a completely different perspective toward the pain and loss I experience in this broken world.

I hope that my story will have a positive influence on your faith walk, but my greater hope is that God will be glorified through this book.

1

OUT OF CONTROL:
THE CROSSROADS OF FAITH

"My God, my God, why have You forsaken me? Far from my deliverance are the words of my groaning. Oh my God, I cry by day, but You do not answer; And by night, but I have no rest."
Psalm 22:1-2

Friday, July 23, 2010

*I*t was midmorning, but it felt like time had stood still. I was supposed to be in the office, but I'd decided to work from home. As much as I tried to complete my assignment, I just couldn't focus. I was lost in time, simply staring at my screen. I called my manager in New York and told her I had to take another day off work.

Anne responded with such compassion, *"Oh Kevin, I'm so sorry. Take as much time as you need. We have everything covered here at work. You're such a good man, and you don't deserve to experience something like this."*

As a tear rolled down my cheek, I thanked her for understanding and told her I was trying as hard as I could to move

1

forward, but the pain was just too much. I truly didn't know what to do next. All I knew is that I wanted to be free from this awful sadness.

In an attempt to get my mind off the pain, I called my dad to see if he wanted to go kayaking. He and I have always enjoyed canoeing and kayaking together ever since I was a child, and I needed to get my mind off things. My hope was that a father-son activity would do the trick—at least for a brief moment in time. It had been two weeks since I'd received the news, and I hadn't been able to stop the thoughts that were haunting me.

I'm not sure how much time had passed, but my dad's knock on the door snapped me out of my numb daze—I'd just been staring at the ravine in my backyard. I'm sure my sadness was apparent, even to him, because as soon as Dad walked in he said, "Kevin, I wish I could take this pain away from you. We are all hurting with you," and gave me a hug.

On our hour-long drive to Clearfork Reservoir, I don't recall talking very much to Dad. It was all I could do to keep from breaking down in tears. We finally arrived and put our kayaks on the water, but after about five minutes, I wanted to go back home. As much as I desired to get my mind off things, I had already missed the comfort that home brings—even if it was a sad, lonely comfort, it was still familiar.

After drifting for a while, I decided to paddle ahead of Dad. I experienced peace and quiet as I floated atop the water, but then it happened. Tears began to fill in my eyes. I desperately tried to focus on something else, so I quickly grabbed my fishing pole, threw out my line, and began trolling for bass. Fishing was one of my favorite outdoor activities, but in this moment, even my favorite past time couldn't keep me from the pain. And in an instant, everything broke loose. I couldn't keep it together any longer. I wept.

As the tears poured down my face, I began to paddle even farther ahead of Dad. I didn't want him to see me this way. Not that he'd ever taught me to hold back emotion. In fact, it was just the opposite. One of the many life lessons I had learned from both my mom and dad was that expressing emotion is healthy for the soul. But for some reason, I didn't want him to see me filled with such sorrow. I was experiencing the lowest point of my life, and I just wanted to be alone.

As I floated along in my kayak with tears streaming down my face, I began to doubt the promises of God I had once believed, and I recognized that I was at a crossroads in my faith. For the first time, I was forced to deal with the challenging questions about God firsthand. Is God really sovereign? Is He even real? This was no longer a casual discussion over a cup of coffee or a philosophical teaching during a Wednesday night Bible study. My situation was real, and I was presented with a decision to believe God is faithful to His Word or to walk away from my faith altogether. I couldn't believe where my mind was taking me because, for most of my life, I had simply accepted what the Bible said as truth. Now I was experiencing something firsthand that appeared to contradict the truth of the Bible and who God says He is.

I couldn't understand why God would allow something so awful into my life, why He would allow sin to prevail, or why He would allow my wife of twelve years to leave me. After all, if God is sovereign and hates divorce as the Bible states in Malachi 2:16, then why would He allow my marriage to fall apart? This is something I did not want, and yet it was something I was being forced to endure. I loved Alyson, and I couldn't understand why she was choosing to leave me. She was breaking our marriage covenant, and I was left behind to carry the burden. Not only was I experiencing betrayal from my wife, I also felt betrayed by God. Confined to my kayak with my dad in the distance and no one else in sight, I looked up to the sky and told God, "I don't know if I believe in You anymore."

* * *

Looking back at the lowest moment of my life, I recognize that I was in a situation that was out of my control. I could do nothing to change my circumstances, and I just wanted the pain to go away. Suffering, whether it be physical, emotional, or psychological, is something that no one desires, and we all possess a natural defense mechanism to avoid it. We are designed to recognize pain as a threat, so we take preventative measures to increase our odds at survival. We will do whatever it takes to make the pain go away, and in almost every case, we want the pain gone immediately.

THREE KINDS OF SUFFERING

Suffering exists in three different varieties, and everyone will encounter all three at some point in life. In some cases, we are able to make a conscious decision to engage in pain. In other situations, we can take preventative measures to avoid suffering. But arguably, the most difficult, the most painful, and the ugliest kind of suffering comes to us without any warning and will remain in our presence until the sorrow decides to leave on its own terms. This suffering comes unplanned, unanticipated, and will change us forever—for better or worse.

The first kind of suffering is **planned suffering**. In this type of suffering, we make a conscious decision to initiate pain. We choose to suffer because we understand the payoff that will result from it, and we measure our planned suffering in terms of cost/benefit. In general, planned suffering is used to improve ourselves mentally, physically, or emotionally. For example, obtaining an advanced college degree, starting a new business, losing weight, purchasing a new home, and raising a family all require sacrifice. We sacrifice time, money, competing desires, and sometimes even relationships to achieve the goals that we value. Those who become successful in planned suffering are not only rewarded for achieving their goals, but they also develop highly sought-after skills such as discipline, motivation, and focus. In most cases, this type of suffering is voluntary, and a person can choose to end the suffering or continue until the goal is achieved.

But not all suffering can be entered into voluntarily. Poor decisions will lead us down the path of **consequential suffering**, where we have no one to blame but ourselves. This type of suffering is usually avoidable, yet we have a desire within us to play Russian roulette with this type of consequential suffering. We have somehow convinced ourselves that participating in something that God has declared "off limits" is better than the pain it will bring. We measure this kind of suffering in terms of risk/reward, and for some reason, we believe the risk is worth the reward. In reality, our reward (the object of desire) will never measure up to the pain of the consequences. Our distorted reason whispers to us, "I don't want to suffer, but I'll engage in something that *might* bring suffering because of the pleasure offered." The drug abuser suffers from the isolation and destruction of addiction. The food abuser suffers from obesity and chronic health ailments from making poor eating decisions. People who seek pleasure in pornography will suffer from a lack of sexual satisfaction. Consequential suffering has been going on ever since the serpent deceived Adam and Eve, and the same truth remains—mankind will suffer the consequences of satisfying desires that do not align with God's character, will, and plan. We may not experience the consequences in real terms immediately, but every poor choice is guaranteed to take us one step farther away from our relationship with God because we are choosing a different path than His. Simply put, we cannot expect to receive God's best from making a poor choice.

Consequential suffering can be extremely intense. Depending on the severity, the person could be forced to live with the consequences for life. The sadness, regret, and guilt that come from this type of suffering can be more than one can handle. People wishing to escape from this type of suffering may begin to look for outlets to cope with the negative feelings, but left to their own devices, they will never find rest or relief. It is only through accepting responsibility for one's poor choice and turning toward God's forgiveness that a person will begin to experience relief. Still, relief may take a significant amount of time before healing is fully recognized. In consequential suffering, people also have the ability to learn from their failures and begin to understand that God's commandments are designed to give freedom and protect mankind from the consequences of sin. When faced with temptation, they will have the ability to resist temptation because they know that God's way is best. They will no longer experience the prison of sin, and they will glorify God by choosing His way. As a matter of fact, consequential suffering can provide an opportunity for the person to grow in self-discipline, similar to planned suffering, but the real benefit is realigning oneself again to God.

The last kind of suffering is arguably the most difficult kind of suffering to endure. It's the suffering that no one can anticipate. People who experience this kind of suffering firsthand will be brought to their knees in sorrow. What makes this kind of suffering so painful is that it comes without warning, and it is no respecter of persons. It is unplanned, and in most cases, there are no answers that will justify the pain of **tragic suffering**. The terrorist attacks on the World Trade Center, natural disasters, cancer, innocent victims of abuse, paralysis, birth defects, the death of a child, an unexpected loss of a loved one—these are just a few examples of tragic suffering. The suffering is harsh, enduring it is extremely painful, and in most cases, the innocent are left with no answers to justify the pain. People who experience this type of suffering are victims of outside forces such as intentional evil, accidental circumstances, or laws of nature.

When examining the three different types of suffering, it's easy to see that with planned suffering, we receive a payoff, and consequential suffering can allow us to learn from our mistakes. But in many cases with tragic suffering, we do not see any reason for undergoing this type of suffering. Additionally, the person does not intentionally initiate the tragedy nor is it a consequence of a poor choice. Victims of tragic suffering spend years searching for answers, but none can be found. Unlike planned suffering and consequential suffering, tragic suffering cannot be measured in any sort of economic terms such as cost/benefit or risk/reward. The measurement of tragedy is only in terms of loss. It is sorrow that seeks its prey and takes up residence for an undetermined timeframe. The person can't escape it and is left saying, "I don't see any good in this suffering, and I want it to go away."

OUR NATURAL RESPONSE TO SUFFERING

Here is one of the underlying beliefs of our American culture: anything worthwhile will require some level of pain to achieve. But truth be told, most everyone, if given the opportunity, would prefer to choose the path of least resistance to achieve the same goal. If presented with the choice between years of exercise to maintain a healthy body or achieving the same level of physical fitness without enduring the time or effort, most everyone would choose the achievement without the pain. In other words, given the opportunity, people will generally choose to avoid pain.

Humans are designed to recognize pain as a threat, so we take preventative measures to increase our odds at survival. Pain avoidance is perfectly natural, and our bodies are excellent machines when it comes to protecting ourselves from pain. Pain is a defense mechanism that screams, "DANGER! PROTECT YOURSELF!" Our bodies respond so quickly to pain that we don't even need to think about it. Our reflexes take over in a matter of milliseconds, and as quickly as we identify the pain, we try to get away from it. Anyone can test this theory by taking a stopwatch, sticking a finger in a light socket, and recording how long it takes to pull out the finger. For the record, I don't recommend anyone actually attempting this, but my guess is the one who attempts such a feat will pull back that finger faster than the time it takes to start and stop the timer!

Avoiding emotional pain is similar to avoiding physical pain, but it's a lot more complicated. Emotional pain would fade quickly if we could bring our loved ones back to life, extract diseases out of bodies, force paralyzed limbs to move, or hold our spouses in our arms until they promise not to leave. The list goes on and on, but the outcomes are the same—certain types of pain cannot be avoided, so our only option is to endure.

The very definition of suffering means to endure pain. As discussed earlier, we might be willing to suffer because we believe the pain will eventually lead to a greater good, goal, or purpose. In this case, we subconsciously rationalize pain in the following terms: as pain increases, the payoff should also increase; otherwise, do not endure the pain. This logic works well in planned suffering because we can determine whether or not we want to engage in the pain. We are in control of the situation. This rationale also helps us through consequential suffering because we learn that our actions yield consequences. However, excessive consequential suffering or unnecessary tragic suffering tend to appear to us as unfair and unjust.

When suffering is excessive or unjust, our natural reaction is to take matters into our own hands. We pursue "pain avoidance" in the hopes of eliminating the pain. Sometimes, we will try so hard to avoid pain that we will begin to make poor choices. Drugs, alcohol, hobbies, entertainment, TV, movies, sports, exercise, material possessions, and misusing relationships are just a few examples of how people attempt to medicate the pain. Unfortunately, all of these examples either are, or can lead to, unhealthy ways of dealing with the pain. And an even more damaging result can arise when we begin to doubt God in the midst of our suffering. This doubt might begin subtly by simply asking the question, "Why God? Why me?" or it may become so extreme as to doubt His existence. Regardless of the degree, we turn away from God with every thought of disbelief.

THE FUTILITY OF ASKING WHY

Just as pulling our finger from an electrical outlet is a natural physical reflex, our natural cognitive reflex to unjust suffering is to ask the question, "Why?" Thoughts flood our minds such as, "Why God? Why did You allow this to happen? If You are all-powerful, why didn't You stop it? If You are a God of love, why are You allowing something so painful in my life?"

Even though posing questions to God is a natural cognitive reflex, it is a futile exercise because logical answers cannot heal emotional wounds. For example, the Bible has already provided the following explanation for why we experience unjust suffering here on earth:

Pain and sorrow are the result of a fallen world that's been broken since the time of Adam and Eve. The fall of man altered the course of this world in ways that our human minds cannot even comprehend. Evil, injustice, disease, natural disasters, and death are all a result of the fall of man, and our world has been broken ever since. Can God fix all of this? The answer is an absolute—Yes!

Before time began, God already knew mankind would rebel against Him and this world would suffer from the brokenness brought forth from rebellion. Knowing this, He established a perfect plan to redeem this fallen world before He even created it. He's been in the process of redeeming the world to its original state since the day He made animal skins for Adam and Eve to cover their nakedness, and He will continue to reinstate the world to its intended design. In other words, He has been redeeming the world, He is currently redeeming the world, and He will continue to redeem the world until it is fully accomplished. But this will be completed on His timetable—not ours. Until then, we will continue to experience the aftermath of suffering that comes from living in a broken world.

Even though the above explanation is absolutely true and answers the question as to why we suffer, people who are in the midst of significant suffering will continue to feel pain even if they understand this explanation. Logic may sooth the mind, but the soul is comprised of more than mere human intellect. And suffering reaches deep into the soul, where logical explanations and head knowledge fall short of complete healing.

LOGICAL ANSWERS CANNOT HEAL EMOTIONAL WOUNDS.

Asking God "Why?" can also be dangerous because this questioning can lead to unbelief. Once doubt sets in, it is not long before we begin thinking God has made a mistake. In doing so, we usurp God by attempting to sit on His throne of judgment. What started out as an innocent question in the midst of our pain has now transitioned to sin because we have come to the conclusion that we know better than God. So, instead of asking, "Why God?" we should be asking, "What do You want me to do next, so that I may eventually overcome this suffering?" By shifting our thought pattern, we move ourselves from the wrongful place of sitting on God's judgment seat to our rightful place of kneeling before His throne.

ABANDONED WITH AN EMOTIONAL WOUND

Looking back on that July kayaking trip, I couldn't believe what was running through my mind. I had come to the point where I was thinking about abandoning God. Many people describe "rock bottom" in different ways, but for me it's when a person experiences helplessness and hopelessness simultaneously. I had never truly experienced "rock bottom" until that moment, and I knew it without a doubt—this was the lowest point of my life. When I was twelve years old, I had made the decision to follow Jesus and allow Him to be the Lord of my life. Throughout my faith journey, I had always assumed that He would take care of me. Sure, I knew that life would bring sorrow, but I trusted that God would bring me through the sorrow. Twenty-six years later, I was now faced with the reality that Alyson was leaving me and God wasn't doing anything about it. While I knew there were very few guarantees in life, I'd always thought I had two guarantees: my salvation and my marriage to Alyson. After all, we'd made a commitment to each other until death do us part. Now that my marriage was beyond repair, I began to seriously question the other so-called "guarantee"—my salvation.

Up to that point, I had truly believed that as long as I remained committed to God, He would protect me from the brokenness in the world—especially from something like divorce. From the moment I committed my life to Christ, I tried my very best to sin less and serve God more in the hope that my life would turn out well.

I was a model student in grade school, went to college and graduated with a finance degree, married Alyson, had a lovely daughter Meredith, and pursued a highly successful career. I had done my best at practicing the Christian faith, and now all of that effort appeared to be a waste of time. I had spent thousands of hours studying the Bible, praying, obeying God's laws, serving regularly, and giving consistently. It seemed that the results of this discipline generally worked out well for me. I knew right from wrong after all the years of growing up in the church, and I was concerned about making this world a better place. All I had to do was live by the golden rule—do unto others as I would have them do unto me. This philosophy made sense to me, and I implemented the golden rule without much difficulty.

While I knew I wouldn't be immune to misfortune, I definitely thought that God would give me the desires of my heart if I delighted in Him (Psalms 37:4). I also believed that if I asked for anything in Jesus' name, God would give it to me (John 16:23). All I wanted was a nice and wholesome life. I didn't need to "have it all", and I wasn't asking God for anything excessive. I had witnessed many non-Christians living the good and nice life, so why couldn't I have the same? Experience had taught me that working hard and living a morally upright life would reap rewards in the long run. But with the demise of my marriage, new thoughts entered my mind. Who needs God if this is how He treats His children? I concluded that if my childhood salvation experience was real then I was guaranteed to go to heaven when I died. But if my salvation experience was false, then I wasn't about to waste any more time following a God Who wasn't faithful to His word.

In the midst of my suffering, I believed that God was either absent in this situation or had abandoned me. I couldn't figure out why He wasn't answering my prayers for Alyson to remain in our marriage. I'd confessed to both Alyson and God that I was willing to change anything in order to prevent the divorce, but my petitions appeared to fall on deaf ears. I couldn't believe this was how God was going to repay me. I had been begging Him for weeks to change Alyson's mind. If He is all-powerful, my simple request should have been easy for Him. If God is actively involved in this world, why wouldn't He make this one change? If marriage is a reflection of Christ's relationship with the church, why would He allow my marriage to fall apart after I'd been committed to Him? I had never prayed so hard in my life for God to bring Alyson back to me, and all I seemed to receive from my heart-felt prayers was an empty silence.

When I reflect on that moment, I can see that my emotional despair overwhelmed me. I was thrown into a terrible situation that I couldn't control and all I wanted was for the pain to go away.

* * *

No one is exempt from tragic suffering. Believers and non-believers alike are fully exposed to this kind of suffering; the Bible doesn't offer any immunity. In the midst of our sorrow, we come to the end of ourselves, unable to rely on our knowledge, ability, and effort to eliminate the pain from emotional wounds. Admired characteristics such as self-discipline, self-determination, and self-motivation fail us. Everything is out of control, and we fall to our knees at the crossroads of our faith wondering which way to turn. Will we continue to believe God and take steps of faith even if we don't understand or will we turn down the path that looks familiar and seems right from our perspective? One path tells us to endure the pain, while the other takes us down the path of pain avoidance.

As I sat in my kayak on that July afternoon, I had come to the crossroads of my faith, and I didn't know which path I was going to take. In the quiet suspension, as I floated atop the water, I found myself drowning in the empty silence of brokenness as the wind drifted me wherever it pleased.

* * *

Questions for Reflection:

1. Have you experienced a crisis that has totally broken your heart? How have you responded to that crisis?

2. How do you view God in the context of suffering?

3. What does our response to suffering tell us about ourselves and our relationship with God?

2

I DID ALL THE RIGHT THINGS: ISN'T LIFE SUPPOSED TO BE OK?

"Now this I say, he who sows sparingly will also reap sparingly, and he who sows bountifully will also reap bountifully."
II Corinthians 9:6

"But the Lord is faithful and He will strengthen and protect you from the evil one."
II Thessalonians 3:3

APRIL 1984

I'll never forget the day I committed my life to Jesus. It was a Wednesday night, and our entire family was at church. Mom went to choir practice, and while Dad wasn't in the choir, he came along to help out with whatever needed to be done or to participate in some committee meeting. Spending our Wednesday nights as a family at St. John's was as common as going to Sunday morning church.

Since there weren't many children who were our age, my sister Angie and I would typically hang out on our own until

17

Mom and Dad finished what they needed to do at church. On this particular Wednesday night, I passed by a picture in the church basement. It was the classic artwork Christ at Heart's Door by Warner Sallman. My Sunday School teacher, Brenda, had recently taught my sister and me about the imagery contained within the picture: Christ's luminosity representing the light of the world, the heart shape on the doorway, the overgrowth representing the sin that consumes us, the clearing of that overgrowth and beauty of life that Christ brings, the absence of the door handle requiring the door of our hearts to be opened from within, and the caption of Revelation 3:20 where Jesus says, "Here I am! I stand at the door and knock. If anyone hears my voice and opens the door, I will come in and eat with that person, and they with me." I don't know of another picture that captures the hope that the Christian faith provides. Even to this day, whenever I see the picture, I'm reminded of Jesus' desire to be our Lord combined with His willingness to give us the free will to choose Him as our Lord. Without the freedom to choose, it is impossible for love to exist.

As I passed by the picture, I paused to study it further. I began thinking about what Brenda had taught me, not only about the picture itself, but all of her lessons about who Jesus is and how we can have assurance of eternal life with Him after we die. I don't recall how long I stared at that picture pondering these things, but suddenly, I was overwhelmed. I knew I didn't want to be separated from God, and I wanted Jesus to be the Lord of my life. I immediately ran to find Dad and told him that I didn't want to go to Hell and wanted Jesus to save me. He asked me if I wanted to talk to Pastor Jim about this, and I remember tears rolling down my face as I talked to the pastor. I still remember his warmth and compassion as he shared how I could be sure to have eternal life with God. After our conversation, Pastor Jim and I prayed together. That was the moment I asked Jesus to be my Savior.

Pastor Jim was gentle in spirit, yet he made it very clear he did not subscribe to all the traditions of the Methodist denomination. For one, he believed deeply in believer's baptism, and he openly preached about baptism by immersion—much to the dislike of several people in our small church. Sadly, some people actually became angry with Pastor Jim for promoting Biblical baptism. Even as a twelve-year-old child, it was clear to me that Jesus commanded baptism; it is something we do when we decide to follow Jesus, and it's performed by complete immersion. At the time, I couldn't understand why people blindly followed a church tradition where baptism was reduced to sprinkling water on an infant's head. Now as an adult, I have learned that anyone can fall into the trap of following non-biblical traditions. We are all susceptible to following church traditions without giving much thought as to whether or not it is actually Biblical. We mean well but have been misled, and in some cases, we become blind to the truth so clearly displayed in the Bible.

Pastor Jim baptized me a couple weeks after that transformational Wednesday night. However, I had to be baptized at another local church because my Methodist church didn't provide the means for baptism by immersion. Dad supported me in my decision and came to be a part of that important day. Mom stayed home.

* * *

From the time I committed my life to Christ in 1984 up to the point when Alyson left me, my spiritual journey had been what I would call the typical Christian experience. I'd always held closely to my faith ever since I was a child. My younger sister and I grew up in a home with loving parents who made sure we understood the importance of worshiping God. We attended St. John's United Methodist Church every Sunday in the small town of Columbus Grove located in rural northwest Ohio. My mom served faithfully as the church organist, and my dad was very active in various church roles. Attendance on a good Sunday would reach over one hundred people, but typically we would average around seventy or so. My younger sister and I represented the entire youth group on most Sundays. While I'd always wished to go to a church that had other children my age, I am very grateful for the people at St. John's who invested time and energy into teaching the Gospel to Angie and me. Our church was over one hundred years old, and my sister and I were the fourth generation on my mom's side of the family who made St. John's our home church. Like most small town churches in the U.S., St. John's was predictable, dependable, and rich with tradition.

Following my commitment to Christ, I rested in the absolute assurance that God had forgiven me because Jesus' sacrifice had completely covered my sins—past, present, and future. Not only was I forgiven, but He'd also given me a new life and the gift of the Holy Spirit. Since Jesus paid the death penalty for my sins, I would never have to worry about being eternally separated from God. My decision to accept Christ as my Savior was by faith, and I do not question it. I've experienced the Holy Spirit working inside of me throughout my life, transforming me into a new creation just as the Bible promises. I know without a doubt that I am His and He is mine. This assurance of salvation brings a peace that transcends all understanding.

Still, it wasn't always this way. At different times along my spiritual walk, I wondered if my salvation was, in fact, legitimate and real. I believe this is something most Christ followers struggle with on occasion. How can we know for sure if we are in good standing with God? If my salvation is by faith, how much faith is required? How do I know if I've received salvation? These are some questions that commonly plague many believers.

THE TRUTH: WHAT THE SCRIPTURES TEACH ABOUT SALVATION

At some point in life, everyone must honestly reflect upon and determine if he or she has received God's gift of salvation.

So, what does Scripture say about this precious gift?

- Jesus Himself makes the claim that He is the only way to God, and no other way exists (John 14:6).

- God has provided the way for salvation through His Son Jesus by having Him pay the penalty of our sin (II Corinthians 5:21).

- We cannot earn salvation by our own efforts because we all fall short of God's righteousness (Ephesians 2:8-9).

- This reconciled relationship to God was initiated first by God, not man (Romans 5:8).

- Salvation is an opportunity God gives to every person, and God doesn't want anyone to perish (II Peter 3:9).

So, how is one saved?

- Our only response to God's gracious gift of salvation is to receive His gift through faith (Ephesians 2:8).

21

- We are to confess with our mouths and believe in our hearts that Jesus is Lord (Romans 10:9-10).

THOSE BIG BIBLE TERMS: JUSTIFICATION AND SANCTIFICATION

After we confess with our mouths and believe in our hearts (Romans 10:9-10), we are justified (Romans 3:24) and reborn spiritually (John 3:5-6). This first part of salvation, called **justification,** means that God has removed our guilt and punishment for sin while at the same time making us righteous through Christ's atoning sacrifice. That is to say, we are now in right standing with God and are no longer guilty before a holy God. Our justification also marks our spiritual birthday. On our spiritual birthday, our old "self" has died with Christ's death on the cross, we've been made alive in Christ, and we're sealed with the Holy Spirit (Ephesians 1:13).

But salvation is not only a one-time event—it is also a lifelong journey of following Christ (Luke 9:23-24), becoming more Christ-like (John 15:5), glorifying God (I Corinthians 6:20) and telling others about God's free gift of salvation (Matthew 28:19-20). This second part of salvation is called **sanctification,** and it's the progressive work of God transforming the believer into the image of His likeness.

Even though God is working in us, Scripture reminds us that, until we are united with Christ in Heaven, we must also work out our salvation with fear and trembling (Philippians 2:12). Just as we work out physically to strengthen our muscles, we must also work out spiritually to strengthen our faith. However, "working out" our salvation should never be confused with "working for" our salvation. We can do nothing to earn our salvation—it is a free gift from God alone. Performance-based Christianity (i.e. working for salvation) is unbiblical and stands in opposition to God's grace. When we begin to believe our conduct somehow determines our status with God, then we are attempting to work apart from God's grace. This view of "faith" is grounded in us and doesn't involve God. If we have been truly justified by God, we will begin to be changed by God, and this begins the life-long sanctification process. Thus, we work out our salvation as God also works in us.

THE AFTERMATH OF MY SALVATION

From the time I committed my life to Jesus at age twelve, I followed the basic philosophy that many American Christians have been taught. Once we accept Christ, we do our best at sinning less and serving God more with the hope that our lives will turn out okay. We possess a general understanding that sorrow and sadness are bound to arise, but all in all, our goal is to get through this life here on earth as pain-free as possible. So, we do our best at living the American Dream of pursuing such things as happiness, comfort, and success. We recognize that nothing is inherently sinful in pursuing these goals, so we pursue them with all of our knowledge, ability, and effort. At the same time, we continue to do our best to live a morally upright and virtuous life and make sure we do our best at serving God both in and

> I FOLLOWED THE BASIC PHILOSOPHY THAT MANY AMERICAN CHRISTIANS HAVE BEEN TAUGHT. ONCE WE ACCEPT CHRIST, WE DO OUR BEST AT SINNING LESS AND SERVING GOD MORE WITH THE HOPE THAT OUR LIVES WILL TURN OUT OKAY.

outside of the church. We recognize that God has provided us with so much, so we want to show our gratitude by focusing on spiritual disciplines such as studying the Bible, praying, obeying the commandments, attending church faithfully, serving, giving, and sharing the Gospel with others. Like so many other American Christians, I focused a lot of time and effort on actively practicing these spiritual disciplines.

STUDYING THE BIBLE

Shortly after becoming a Christian, I began reading the Bible, and I didn't even need my parents to reinforce this behavior—I just did it. I found great comfort in God's promises, and I simply believed everything in the Bible was true without ever really questioning it. My believing God's Word to be true and applying it to my life created a path for me to grow spiritually. I actually enjoyed reading my Bible when I was a child and didn't see it as something I was required to do. It was not uncommon for me to set aside time to read Scripture, memorize verses that were important to me, and spend time thinking about God's Word. I understood the importance of Bible study and made it a priority.

As I grew into a young adult, I began studying particular Scriptures to help get me through life's challenges. When I was feeling inadequate or insecure, I would search for verses that reminded me of who I was in Christ. When I needed comforting, I found verses that ministered to my heart. When I was worried, I read verses about peace and contentment. I took the popular Christian view that the Bible is our playbook for life, and I did my best to consult it as I made key decisions.

PRAYING REGULARLY

My prayer life as a new believer consisted mainly of prayers such as, "Lord, help me get over this sickness. Protect me from harm and keep me safe. Please let this girl like me. I messed up—please don't let me get in trouble. Help me do well on my test." My prayer life seemed to be filled with "bless me" prayers where I asked God to help me achieve a goal, receive something good, or avoid something harmful. Sure, I gave thanks to God, but secretly, I did so in the hope that He would answer my next prayer or bless me with the next big item on my wish list. I never confessed my ulterior motive to Him—it was my little secret, and I didn't want Him to find out.

As I matured into an adult, I discovered that prayer could be more than a wish list. I enjoyed spending quiet time with God, meditating on a Scripture, or simply giving thanks to Him for all of His blessings. I routinely prayed for others and witnessed God answering those prayers of physical healing, overcoming adversity, and growing spiritually. Not every prayer was answered the way I expected, and this sometimes confused me or left me with a tinge of doubt. Eventually, as I grew in my faith, I learned that God was not obligated to answer all of my prayers the way I wanted.

Even though I prayed for others, gave thanks to God, and meditated on His Word, I still spent a considerable amount of time asking Him for things. These weren't always material things, even though it wasn't uncommon for me to ask for a pay raise, job promotion, or bigger house. I didn't necessarily need more things, just *nicer* things, and I didn't see any harm in asking since I'd always been generous with what God gave me. What I wanted even more than nice things was to live in comfort and security. I didn't want to worry about finances, live in a dangerous neighborhood, or lack basic needs. I wanted my family to live in a nice house in a nice neighborhood with a nice school system and afford nice clothes and nice food, and drive nice cars. Much to my surprise, I received all of these things in abundance.

OBEYING THE COMMANDMENTS

I never got into much trouble growing up. I was one of those kids who did a pretty good job following the rules. Sure, I broke rules from time to time, particularly in high school and college, but overall, I would describe myself as a rule follower. Since I liked following the rules, obeying God's commandments seemed to come fairly natural to me. Jesus Himself said, "If you love me, you will obey my commandments." I loved Jesus, so I wanted to please Him by obeying the commandments as best as I could.

Knowing that I was doing my best to follow God's law made me feel good, yet I hated the feeling when I failed—especially if it was something I knew was wrong ahead of time and deliberately disobeyed anyway. Guilt and shame were something that fell heavy on me. Even though I knew God had forgiven me of all my sins—past, present, and future—I didn't want to disappoint God by breaking His rules.

As I matured into an adult, married Alyson, and had a family, I continued to obey God's law, so I could be an exceptional husband and father. I also tried to follow the rules because I wanted to be a model citizen and manager at work. I obeyed the commandments out of a sense of duty and obligation, because I wanted to represent the Christian faith and myself well. If I professed to be a Christian, I knew others would be watching my actions under a microscope, so I figured I needed to be on my best behavior all of the time.

ATTENDING CHURCH AND SERVING

For as long as I can remember, attending church was simply a part of life. There was no debate, no question, and no decision whether or not we felt like going—we went every Sunday. I'm so grateful that Mom and Dad made church a priority, and for the most part, I liked going even though my sister and I were the only kids who came consistently.

When I moved down to Columbus as a college student at The Ohio State University, my church attendance became less consistent. I would typically bounce back and forth between King Avenue United Methodist Church and Lane Avenue Baptist Church (LABC). I went to King Avenue simply because it was the same denomination as my home church. Craig, my roommate, was a Baptist and attended Lane Avenue on the Sundays he didn't travel home for the weekend, and I would tag along with him.

After college, church attendance became more consistent, and I eventually made LABC my church home. Alyson and I were married there in 1998, and our daughter Meredith was dedicated there in 2001. We remained active members at LABC until 2006 when we moved north of Columbus and found Worthington Christian Church. Similar to how I grew up, Alyson, Meredith, and I went to church every Sunday without a second thought.

Actively serving at church was also second nature to me because of how my parents modeled it in their lives. In my early years at LABC, I taught the college and career Sunday school group, and for eight years, I served faithfully. I taught three different Sunday school groups, served on the properties committee, became a deacon, served as church treasurer, and participated in almost every church initiative and program.

By the time Alyson and I transferred to Worthington Christian Church in 2006, I was burned out from serving at LABC. My career was also very demanding at this time, and I recognized that my spiritual connection with God was distant. Worthington became a safe haven for me where I truly felt like I could reconnect with my Savior and experience spiritual and emotional healing. As a result, I served in a much smaller capacity at Worthington Christian. Instead of holding actual positions within the church, I limited my service to volunteering for different programs and initiatives that would fit within my demanding work schedule along with my other roles of being a husband to Alyson and a father to Meredith.

GIVING GENEROUSLY

When I first received an allowance, I began giving a portion of what I made to the church. I don't remember it being a full tithe (10%), but I did give something. When I became an adult, I made the commitment to tithe consistently. I wouldn't always give my entire 10% to the church, as I gave to other non-profits and faith-based initiatives also.

I knew that tithing was a fundamental part of what it means to be a Christian. I always viewed giving 10% of my income as my duty, not because it put me in a better standing with God, but rather, because I was giving back to God the resources He'd given me. It was really a gesture of appreciation for what He'd provided.

I also understood the Bible's promises of blessing regarding our tithes: "'Bring the whole tithe into the storehouse, so that there may be food in My house, and test Me now in this,' says the Lord of hosts, 'if I will not open for you the windows of heaven and pour out for you a blessing until it overflows'" (Malachi 3:10). So, in my mind, tithing was not optional.

SHARING THE GOSPEL

Evangelism was an area where I never really felt comfortable. I tried various strategies, but none of them really appeared to produce much fruit in terms of people committing their lives to Christ. I tried to view the workplace as my "mission field," but to be honest, I rarely shared my faith with anyone—not verbally anyway. I knew that sharing my faith in the office was a delicate situation that could get me fired, so I needed to use caution when witnessing to others. As a result, instead of facilitating Gospel conversations, I relied on my actions to speak for me. An old saying that many credit to St. Francis states, "Preach the gospel at all times, and if necessary, use words." This inspirational quote appealed to me because I usually felt awkward initiating Gospel conversations. By allowing my actions to speak on my behalf, I figured I could avoid these uncomfortable conversations. If people knew I was a person of integrity, respectful to others, and possessing a good work ethic, then non-believers might see something different in me and ask why my behavior was different from others. I figured once they approached me, then I could share the reason, which was my faith in Christ.

* * *

While I knew I wasn't perfect at practicing spiritual disciplines, I did my very best with what little time my busy schedule allowed, and I was grateful that God's grace covered my imperfections. I figured that as long as God saw my well-intentioned efforts, He would reward me with a life of happiness, comfort, and success. So, I lived by the reaping and sowing principle that Paul illustrated to the church at Corinth because it made sense. As long as I kept up my end of the bargain of sowing for the Lord, I truly believed He would make sure my life turned out okay.

WAIT A SECOND—EVERYTHING IS NOT OK!

Up to the point of Alyson leaving me, I had spent my entire life dedicated to practicing the Christian faith. In doing so, I assumed God would protect me from the evil of this world. I *never* expected to experience a traumatic situation like divorce. As anyone who's experienced divorce knows, it destroys relationships, severs the family unit, erodes trust, increases fear, and creates a significant number of emotional wounds. Because divorce is so terrible, I had expected God to protect me from such an evil because of His promises in Scripture:

- "The Lord will protect you from all evil; He will keep your soul" (Psalms 121:7).

- "The Lord is near to all who call upon Him, to all who call upon Him in truth. He will fulfill the desire of those who fear Him; He will also hear their cry and will save them" (Psalms 145:18-19).

- "But the Lord is faithful, and He will strengthen and protect you from the evil one" (II Thessalonians 3:3).

Even more, I thought my prayers would send God into action to fix my marriage. I desperately wanted Alyson and I to remain married, so I prayed like I'd never prayed before with a heart desperate for God to make things right. And I believed God would answer my prayers since He's stated multiple times in Scripture that our prayers will be answered:

- "Therefore, I say to you, all things for which you pray and ask, believe that you have received them, and they will be granted to you" (Mark 11:24).

- "Whatever you ask in My name, that will I do, so that the Father may be glorified in the Son. If you ask Me anything in my name, I will do it" (John 14:13-14).

- "If you abide in Me, and My words abide in you, ask whatever you wish, and it will be done for you" (John 15:7).

But nothing changed.

All of these Scriptures seemed to indicate that God had promised to protect me from evil and answer my prayers, but my experience was telling me otherwise. The Lord was *not* protecting me from evil. He didn't feel near. He didn't answer my cry. In fact, He was choosing *not* to change my circumstances. I had asked Jesus for my greatest desire, but He didn't fulfill it. And as I reflected on all of the sacrifices I'd made *for God* over the years, I felt cheated. How could He let something this terrible happen to someone like me? I felt alone and abandoned to suffer from an experience that seemed to contradict the promises found in His word. As a result, I began to conclude that the Bible was only partially true, and God only keeps His word some of the time.

* * *

Questions for Reflection:

1. Think of a time when God said, "No" to a prayer request when you desperately wanted a "Yes." Are you still upset with Him for not answering the prayer in the way you wanted?

2. Have you ever experienced a situation that appeared to be inconsistent with Scripture? If so, briefly summarize your experience and then highlight the Scripture(s) that appears to contradict your experience. How did you respond to this contradiction? How did it affect your relationship with God?

3. Have you ever felt abandoned or cheated by God? If so, how did it affect your relationship with Him? Do you believe you have grown closer to Him or further from Him as a result of this experience?

3

THE AMERICAN DREAM: PURSUING THE "GOOD LIFE"

"I can do all things through Him who strengthens me."
Philippians 4:13

SPRING 2009

*A*fter a hard and stressful day at work, I came home and began looking through the mail, and there it was. A letter addressed to me from Capital University Law School. I'd been waiting anxiously for weeks wondering when the letter would come. I opened the letter, and my wish had come true. I was officially accepted into law school!

Words can't express how excited I was. I had spent hundreds of hours preparing for law school: practicing for the LSAT, improving my critical reading skills, actually taking the LSAT, and then going through the lengthy and tedious process of applying to law school. All of the hard work and dedication had paid off, and now I was officially a law school student!

Up to this point in my career, I'd achieved everything I wanted, but corporate life had become unpleasant and somewhat boring. Even though I held a senior management position and had accomplished all of my career goals, I needed a new challenge in life and thought law school was the perfect fit. I'd become increasingly disenchanted with the direction our country was heading, and as a lawyer, I truly believed that I could make a positive change, even if it was a small one.

Deciding to attend law school is not a fly by night decision or one that's made on a whim, especially for someone like myself who'd been out of college for several years. Alyson and I had discussed at length whether or not I should even pursue law school. We both knew that obtaining my J.D. and passing the bar exam would require a significant amount of time and dedication. Alyson worked in the healthcare industry and also had a very successful career, so she could easily relate to my desire to pursue something greater. After weighing the options, we finally agreed that I should pursue law school, and she was very supportive.

When I applied to Capital University Law School in the spring of 2009, only 15% of the applicants were chosen, so I was thrilled to have been selected. I planned on attending part-time, so I could continue working part-time. That way, I could still earn an income while paying for law school. I was very fortunate that Capital was located in downtown Columbus and provided not only a part-time program, but also an evening program that aligned well with my work hours.

From the time I began considering law school to the time I received the acceptance letter, it had been over a two-year process. What weighed heavily on my mind was the time commitment. I knew I would have very little free time, and what little extra time was available, I wanted to spend it with my family. Still, I decided to make the sacrifice because my wife supported me, and I believed I could make a difference in the moral fiber of our community. Most of all, I believed God was on my side, and He would see me through the difficult times. After all, I could do all things through Him who strengthens me. But the struggle of balancing work, school, and family was ever-present and accurately reflected in the following entry from my journal:

SUNDAY, AUGUST 30, 2009

I survived my first week in law school. It was VERY hard, but I really enjoyed it. My only concern right now is how I'm going to be able to sustain this pace for the next three years. I keep telling myself to just take it one day at a time and do my best with what the Lord sets before me. I am very fortunate to be able to work part-time from home because it allows me to feel like I'm more involved with Meredith's life. I get to see her off to school, and I get to be home when she comes home from school. My weekly schedule right now is 25-30 hours of work, 10 hours of class, and 30 hours of study. I'm trying my best to make sure I set aside Sundays to do nothing at all but spend time with Alyson and Meredith. Today, we took a drive to Dawes Arboretum in Newark. It was a beautiful day—almost like fall.

Meredith started the third grade this past Wednesday. On Tuesday evening, Meredith and I took a walk on the trail off Plumb Road that leads to the Alum Creek Reservoir. We had a wonderful time together. Meredith waded in the water searching for rocks and shells, while I relaxed and watched the sun set. As I watched her play in the water, I thought about the fun times I had as a child playing in the creek and enjoying nature. Times are simpler as an eight-year-old.

When we were walking back to the truck, it was almost dark. I could tell Meredith was afraid, and I reassured her that nothing would hurt us. I could immediately sense relief in her demeanor. When we finally arrived at the truck, she told me, "Daddy, I love going on walks with you, and I love talking to you about stuff. I feel like I can talk to you about anything."

I replied, "Meredith, you will never know how good that makes me feel. I love you so much, and I am so thankful that you are my daughter. I couldn't think of a better way for us to spend the last day of summer break together."

"Me too, Daddy."

* * *

That evening was very memorable to me, and honestly, it was a bit of a wake-up call. I realized my pursuit of law school was pulling me away from what I cherished most—my family. I did fairly well at putting up a façade, but on the inside, I was feeling the strain. Being accepted into law school was one of my greatest achievements; however, the strain of attending law school, working in a part-time role as a corporate executive, and being a husband and father took a heavy toll on me. Still, I considered all of my stress and anxiety to be the price I had to pay in order for my family to live the American Dream.

I will never forget that walk with Meredith. Everything within me just wanted to stay with her in that moment and slow down to a simpler way of life. The thought of taking on Jesus' easy yoke and light burden was very appealing, but I had already begun the heavy burden of advancing my career. I felt that turning away now would just make me a quitter. At the risk of burning out, I continued to carry the yoke of achievement, so my family could enjoy the American Dream. For this period of my life, I believed giving up time with my family was the sacrifice I had to make. Once I achieved this goal, I could provide a better life for my family, and we could cherish quality time together while enjoying the nicer things in life.

MY PURSUIT OF HAPPINESS

The passion that led to my successful career and to law school found its roots in the pursuit of the American Dream. Most of us are taught at a very young age that if we set our minds on anything we can achieve it. All we need is an opportunity combined with persistence and determination, and we can create our own destiny. In essence, the American Dream can be summed up in the popular motivational statement, "If you can dream it, you can achieve it."

But in order to "achieve it," a person must be equipped with three qualities: knowledge, ability, and effort. Knowledge can be defined as hearing, processing, and retaining information. Ability can be broken into three categories: physical (ex. strength, agility, coordination, and endurance), mental (ex. self-discipline, motivation, and focus) and social (ex. listening, expression, and communication). Effort is the degree to which we apply ourselves and can be described as having a strong work ethic, persistence, or determination.

Every living person possesses knowledge, ability, and effort at various levels. As a first world country, American culture admires and rewards individuals who possess these attributes and applies them effectively. So, the natural tendency is to teach people at a young age to increase their knowledge as much as possible, improve their abilities, and always put forth their best effort in everything they do. By the time I was in my early twenties, I truly believed I possessed a high degree of knowledge, ability, and effort.

And this provided me with a tremendous amount of confidence while I pursued the American Dream.

I discovered the benefits of applying knowledge, ability, and effort along with the power of planned suffering when I was seventeen. Throughout most of my childhood, I was overweight, and as I entered my teenage years, I became obese. I constantly prayed that God would miraculously make me thin so kids wouldn't tease me and girls would like me. Much to my amazement, He answered my prayer, but He didn't make my struggle miraculously disappear. His plan was to grant me the gifts of discipline, motivation, and focus. All I had to do was make a decision to lose the weight and engage in planned suffering. I had to use these skills to create a lifestyle change that enabled me to lose weight. This lifestyle change was a decision I had to make, and I had to endure suffering to achieve the goal.

Planned suffering meant that I could no longer eat what I wanted. I now had to eat foods that grew in a garden and didn't come in a packaged bag or box. This was a shock to my system! Pizza, hamburgers, and ice cream had to be replaced with salad and fish, and dessert wasn't even an option. I completely eliminated junk food and replaced it with fruits and vegetables. What was worse, I had to measure everything. Portion control was key if I wanted to regulate calories.

Over a period of three months during the summer between my junior and senior year in high school, I lost thirty-five pounds. This success gave me all the motivation I needed, and I ended up losing ninety pounds overall. I went from weighing 270 pounds my junior year down to 180 one year later. Instead of making fun of me, people were complimenting me. I had consciously decided to go through a period of planned suffering because the benefit of being thin was greater than the cost of being obese.

As a result of my weight loss and also graduating from college, I believed that God was on my side. By this time, I'd been a Christian for over ten years, and I had firsthand experience of His working in my life. I began to develop the mindset, "With God on my side, I can achieve anything." Much of this mindset came directly from Philippians 4:13, so I set out to do what any responsible college graduate would do—pursue a good living. I didn't want to waste the talents God had given me, so I began to use my knowledge, ability, and effort to pursue the American Dream. Still, I knew I needed to keep Christ at the center of my life because He was my strength (Psalms 59:17), and I couldn't do anything without Him (John 15:5). So, I set out to pursue the American Dream with the hope that my life would turn out well as I attempted to sin less and serve God more.

THE PURSUIT OF "GOOD AND NICE"

While each of us might possess a slightly different vision of the American Dream, we generally derive our understanding of it from the Declaration of Independence that states, "We hold these truths to be self-evident, that all men are created equal, that they are endowed by their Creator with certain unalienable Rights, that among these are Life, Liberty and the pursuit of Happiness." As an American Christian, I possessed the same point of view as many of my brothers and sisters in Christ when it came to the American Dream. I recognized that God provided all three of these unalienable rights in His Absolute Sovereignty, and I was fortunate enough to live in a country where I could experience the good life free from government oppression while actively pursuing happiness. Thus, my faith was a moral compass that guided me towards a type of happiness that honored God's laws, and most importantly, did not hurt or degrade my fellow citizens. Using the golden rule as the litmus test, I could easily determine if my actions were appropriate. As long as I held myself accountable to consistently applying church disciplines, I could aggressively pursue the good life as long as it stayed within the moral and ethical boundaries of God's commands.

Having this mindset, I knew that any long-lasting or true happiness would not come from doing things that God declared "off limits," such as dishonest gain, self-indulgence, and living in excess. I wanted to honor God by living a life of good, moral integrity, so I recognized that my pursuit of happiness needed to pursue things that were "good" and "nice." I didn't want a lavish lifestyle, but I wanted a nicer lifestyle than the average American. While I didn't want to be considered an elitist who looked down on those who were less fortunate or didn't achieve as much, I did want to pursue a good name for myself—someone who was able to achieve a successful career by doing things the right way. I didn't need the best of everything, but I did want to provide my family with opportunities that I didn't have. From a Biblical standpoint, I couldn't find anything wrong with pursuing these goals because I had my heart set on pursuing them in a way that would honor and glorify God. I concluded that I could have the best of both worlds—a good and nice life here on earth and eternal life with Christ.

My strategy for pursuing happiness could be summarized by the following statement: achieve self-sufficiency through acquisition. Once I achieved self-sufficiency, I would turn my efforts toward accumulating more and more until I reached my goal. My plan didn't really differ too much from the typical white-collar plan for success, which is generally outlined in the following steps:

- Acquire good grades in school
- Acquire a good physique
- Acquire nice clothes
- Acquire a college degree
- Acquire a successful career
- Acquire a good investment and savings strategy
- Acquire nice possessions such as a nice house, nice home furnishings, and a nice car

I began following this plan as a young adult by applying the skills God had given me to achieve my version of the American Dream. I used knowledge from my college education and wisdom from reading the Bible, combined with self-discipline, motivation, focus, and a strong work ethic to pursue happiness, comfort, and success. And it seemed to be working well.

A PLAN WELL EXECUTED

As a child, I rarely had to work hard for good grades in school. For some reason, learning came easily to me, and I was able to earn A's and B's without much effort. If I really applied myself, I could have been a straight A student, but that was never my passion. I always thought time was better spent enjoying life more than trying to achieve perfection. As a child, enjoying life meant spending time outdoors with my friends. I loved playing football with the neighborhood kids, fishing, exploring, and riding my bike. I didn't want any unnecessary studying to interfere with these finer things in life.

Eating healthily and exercising regularly were foreign concepts to me until I finally lost my weight in high school. Once I was able to finally get the weight off, I was able to keep it off because I trained my body to crave healthy foods and physical activity. I recognized how much better I felt when I ate fresh foods in modest proportions, and I enjoyed gaining muscle mass from weightlifting. I constantly reminded myself that junk food, overeating, and muscle atrophy was an "unhealthy cycle" while fresh foods, modest proportions, and exercising was a "healthy cycle." By the time I graduated college, I had packed on almost forty pounds of muscle—weighing in at 205 with less than 10% body fat. This was a complete reversal of my high school years where I weighed in at 275 pounds, ate junk food, and didn't exercise at all.

From a career standpoint, I struggled to figure out what I wanted to do for a living. For the longest time, I wanted to be a park ranger or game warden because I loved the outdoors, especially hunting and fishing. My dad set up a meeting with a game warden so I could ask him some questions about what he liked and disliked about his job. After he talked at length, he asked me, "Why do you want to become a game warden?" When I replied, "I love hunting and fishing, and I want to be connected to the outdoors," he responded, "Just remember, game wardens are busiest when everyone else is hunting and fishing. You might be better off pursuing a white-collar job, so you can make a decent living and take time off to actually hunt and fish." I'll never forget that conversation and his candid advice. It helped shape my career focus, and from that day forward, I began thinking about careers that would provide opportunities for advancement and financial growth.

The problem was—I didn't know what type of career I wanted. As luck would have it, I took an accounting course my senior year in high school and loved it. I always liked working with numbers, and accounting made me feel like I fit in with Corporate America. At the end of the school year, I represented my high school in a local accounting contest and earned second place, which boosted my confidence even more.

Now that I found a career to pursue, it took very little decision making for me to choose The Ohio State University. I always loved the Buckeyes as a child, and I still love the Buckeyes to this day. Not to mention, my mom graduated from OSU, and she did well in preparing me to follow in her footsteps. Our family album contains a picture of me on my first day of kindergarten wearing an OSU t-shirt—I think it might have been my mom's way of giving me a loving nudge toward her alma mater, and I'm glad she did.

During my sophomore year at OSU, I changed majors from accounting to finance. I graduated in 1995 and began eagerly searching for a career. I began working as a bookkeeper for a small local restaurant chain in Columbus, but it really just paid the bills while I searched for something with more career growth opportunities.

In May of 1996, I landed an entry-level job with BISYS Fund Services, a third-party mutual fund service provider. The company was growing at a rapid pace, and in my first eight years at BISYS, I was promoted four times and found myself holding a senior management position as Director of Fund Services Operations. I experienced tremendous career growth and was optimistic that I could continue pursuing a successful career.

FISCALLY RESPONSIBLE ACCUMULATION

When Alyson and I were married in 1998, we were both positioned for successful careers, but since we were starting at the bottom, our salaries were comparable to entry-level positions. We didn't spend a lot of money during those first couple years of marriage because we were paying off college debt, saving for our dream home, and investing long-term for retirement. We followed a natural progression of renting an apartment, renting a house, and then finally purchasing our first home in February of 2000. Even though it was a starter home, we saw it as an investment that we'd use as a stepping-stone to acquire the house we really wanted. We loved looking at houses together and dreaming about the place we'd eventually live in. While we admired the large mansions in the elite parts of Columbus, neither of us saw that as a realistic goal even though we dreamed about it from time to time.

By the time we moved into our first home, our school debt was paid off, so we used the extra money to acquire nicer things. Instead of hand-me-down furnishings, we began purchasing new and improved versions, but we weren't extravagant as we were still planning and saving for our future. In addition, Alyson was pregnant with our first child, so we were beginning to purchase all kinds of baby clothes and gadgets. We fell into the trap nearly all new parents fall into—feeling severely inadequate and overcompensating by purchasing every single baby gadget on the market guaranteed to help new parents successfully raise their first child.

Once Alyson and I set a goal and achieved it, we simply looked to raise the bar another level. We were thankful for what God had provided for us, but once we achieved a financial, career, material, or family goal, we began focusing on how we could raise the bar again. We truly believed we could accomplish all these things through Christ.

> I USED KNOWLEDGE FROM MY COLLEGE EDUCATION AND WISDOM FROM READING THE BIBLE, COMBINED WITH SELF-DISCIPLINE, MOTIVATION, FOCUS, AND A STRONG WORK ETHIC TO PURSUE HAPPINESS, COMFORT, AND SUCCESS.

One of our biggest achievements was purchasing a custom-built home in what seemed to be the perfect location. The county where we moved, just north of Columbus, was the fastest growing in Ohio. Its school district was consistently ranked at the top of Ohio's public schools, and it was in close proximity to where we both worked. Once we had found the perfect location, it didn't take us long to find the perfect lot to build our perfect home. It was a wooded lot in a subdivision near upscale shopping and dining, yet it was also close to parks that provided outdoor activities such as camping, swimming, hiking, fishing, and hunting. We knew immediately that THIS was where we would raise our family. So, we purchased the lot and began building our new custom home.

THE COST OF A DREAM

In 2007, BISYS announced Citigroup was acquiring it. Fortunately, my job was not eliminated as a result of the acquisition. I received a retention bonus to remain with the company. I saw this as a true blessing and used the retention bonus to purchase furnishings for our new home.

However, a corporate event like a merger or acquisition creates a tremendous amount of stress during the integration phase. That stress combined with the rapid pace in which I'd climbed the corporate ladder was beginning to take its toll on me. I worked long hours and became irritable when I came home.

Alyson and I were convinced that I needed to pursue a different career, and we were both willing to make financial sacrifices to do so. We saw this as just another planned suffering, so we could continue to pursue the American Dream. That's when I began searching for other opportunities, which ultimately led me to law school. I prayed extensively over this decision, and I distinctly recall coming to the following conclusion:

> Why wouldn't God want me to become an attorney? Society at large has such a negative view of the legal system. I believe the Lord can use me as a positive influence within the legal system. I know everything there is to know about good conduct, morality, and ethical behavior through my understanding of the Bible and experience of being a Christian for most of my life.

Although I had spent nearly two years preparing for law school, my law school days were short-lived. Just a couple months after my very first semester, I experienced a back injury that literally laid me out on the ground. I tried to press on through the injury using self-discipline, motivation, and focus. But eventually, everything came to a head, and something had to give. I remember the exact moment I decided to withdraw from law school. I was lying on the floor, trying to get some relief from the extreme pain shooting down my sciatic nerve. I was studying for my contracts mid-term and had just finished a conference call for work. I felt ineffective as a father and a husband, and I knew law school had to go. So, before the second semester began, I submitted my request for withdrawal and was very depressed—I felt like a failure. A little voice inside my head was saying that I just didn't try hard enough and I was a quitter. In hindsight, I believe the injury was a blessing in disguise.

Fortunately, I still had my job at Citi, and while I wasn't enthused to be there, I knew it could provide the salary and benefits my family needed to maintain our current lifestyle. I began to accept the fact that our current standard of living was already much higher than most, and I needed to practice being content and grateful for what God had provided.

While the pursuit of the good and nice life had allowed me to achieve my American Dream, this dream came with a price. My career in the banking industry was very stressful and required many hours. It left me feeling disconnected from my family and burned out. I thought law school was the answer, but looking back, I can see that becoming an attorney would have been more of the same stress and long hours. From a spiritual standpoint, God had been feeling increasingly distant over the years, and now He seemed *very* distant. So, I approached my faith like I'd approached the American Dream and applied all of my knowledge, ability, and effort to it—but this time, it wasn't working. I still felt disconnected from God. I was grateful for the material blessings He'd provided, but for some reason, I was craving something more.

* * *

Questions for Reflection:

1. What is your definition of success? Where does your drive for success come from?

2. In what ways are you depending on God to help you achieve the American Dream or some other goal?

3. What has the tendency to consume your thoughts on a daily basis?

4

AMERICAN PHARISEE: BLINDED BY SELF-RIGHTEOUSNESS

"For not knowing about God's righteousness and
seeking to establish their own*, they did not subject*
themselves to the righteousness of God."
Romans 10:3

JULY 2014

I'd wanted to go fishing for quite some time, and today was the perfect morning. The temperature was pleasant, and the sky was a deep blue. I usually prefer a more overcast day for fishing as the clouds tend to cause the fish to be more active. But on this day, I was more concerned with being outside in God's creation than I was about catching fish. Being in the midst of nature has a way of drawing me closer to God. I love the beauty of God's creation, and being alone in the woods really quiets my soul as I can leave behind the hustle and bustle of the world and enter the peace and tranquility that only the outdoors *can provide. Too much time had passed since being outside, and I could tell my body, soul, and spirit were craving it.*

I knew if I had any chance of catching some fish, I needed to get out before the heat of the day. So, I quickly gathered my fishing gear, loaded up the truck, and drove to Alum Creek Reservoir, which is only about a five-minute drive from my house. I pulled my truck off to the side of the road, walked about a quarter mile into the woods, and checked out a fishing hole along the bank of one of the many inlets that carve into the land. Like most fisherman, I have a certain way of doing things, a protocol, when it comes to fishing. Today, I was fishing from the bank, which means throwing a line out for catfish and then using another pole set up with artificial bait to catch bass. The constant casting and retrieving of the artificial bait keeps me occupied while I wait for the catfish. I throw back all the bass and keep the catfish, but only if they are worth my while to fillet as I don't like wasting my time filleting small fish.

Just as I'd anticipated, the high-pressure system that was creating the deep, blue sunny sky was wreaking havoc on my fishing. After about an hour of high-quality fishing from a veteran fisherman, I couldn't even muster a single bite from either line. Certain that my poor luck was due to the weather and not my fishing skills, I decided to rest for a while along the bank. I hooked my line onto my bass rod and leaned it up against a nearby shade tree, but I left my catfish rig in the water just in case of a surprise catch. As my thoughts (and hopes) began to fade about catching fish, I began reflecting on my life and how so much had changed over the last four years since the divorce.

Before the divorce, I had everything a guy could want—I was highly educated, successful, self-motivated, disciplined, conscientious, well liked, and confident in my abilities. I climbed the corporate ladder at a rapid pace for a large corporation. I made a six-figure income, used my money wisely, and was fortunate to possess nice clothes, nice cars, and a nice house. My beautiful wife and daughter rounded out this picture-perfect American Dream. By all accounts, I was considered a model citizen, and people looked up to me. I was often commended for being a hard-worker who was dedicated to performing at the highest levels. From a faith standpoint, other people viewed me as a mature Christian. I was raised in the church, accepted Christ as my Savior at a young age, possessed a keen sense of right and wrong, and desired to live a morally upright life. I volunteered for several roles at church and became a board member for a non-profit faith-based organization.

I strived to be the perfect husband, father, friend, employee, manager, mentor, and citizen for two primary reasons. First, I loved God and wanted to honor Him. I knew that striving to do my best did not earn salvation because it is a gift freely given out of God's gracious love for me. In return for His priceless gift, I wanted to be the very best representation of a Christian. Second, I wanted others to admire my lifestyle, so they would be attracted to the Christian faith. I wanted people to see that it is possible to be a Christian and be a successful leader, highly educated, and enjoy all of the wonderful things in life. The Christian faith is meant for all, not just the lame and downtrodden. By living the ideal life and claiming my faith as the key to it, I would be a living testimony that worldly success, high moral ideals, and the Christian faith were not mutually exclusive. All three could be experienced simultaneously without having to sacrifice one in order to obtain another.

Even though I had successfully achieved all three of these goals before my marriage fell apart, I often sensed something was missing. I was living a virtuous life and doing all the things a Christian should be doing, but I wasn't experiencing *a close connection with God. I felt like most of my spiritual journey was spent going through the motions of being a Christian. The Christian disciplines of studying my Bible, praying, living a morally upright life, attending church, serving, giving generously, and sharing the Gospel felt more like a burden than a blessing. While I'd remained faithful in doing all of these things out of duty and obligation, I wasn't experiencing much of the freedom that is promised to those who are God's children. So, even though I knew my eternal salvation was secure in Christ, I wasn't experiencing the abundant life Jesus discussed in John 10:10.*

Instead of questioning why I wasn't experiencing freedom in Christ, I had just accepted the fact that God felt distant and continued living the best life I knew how. As I sat under that shade tree along the bank of Alum Creek and reflected on my life before the divorce, for the first time, I became aware that God was distant because I was living like an American Pharisee.

* * *

THE ORIGINAL PHARISEES

Pharisees were considered the spiritual elite in Jesus' day. The requirements to become a Pharisee began as a child. For example, they were required to memorize the entire Torah, otherwise known as the first five books of the Bible. They were also strict followers of all the Laws of Moses. They loved following rules so much that they added numerous laws for the nation of Israel to follow. Pharisees held themselves to the highest of religious standards and took pride in their pious living. Some sources say the term "Pharisee" actually means "separated" from what is unclean and unholy, and, they looked down on anyone who was ordinary and even disregarded people with birth defects or disease. Pharisees enjoyed a high status in their world, and it came with many benefits. They loved the attention and approval they received along with the respect from virtually everyone. Even more, they enjoyed being the leaders because they got to call the shots. Strictly speaking, Pharisees did all the right things for all the wrong reasons.

Jesus had a real problem with these people and confronted them on many occasions. In Matthew 23, Jesus exposes the hypocrisy of the Pharisees because they held such high standards for others to follow, yet even the Pharisees couldn't live up to them. In Matthew 15, Jesus quotes the prophet Isaiah to the Pharisees: "This people honor Me with their lips, but their heart is far away from Me."

> I BECAME AWARE THAT GOD WAS DISTANT BECAUSE I WAS LIVING LIKE AN AMERICAN PHARISEE.

Later in the chapter, Jesus went on to say, "Do you not understand that everything that goes into the mouth passes into the stomach, and is eliminated? But the things that proceed out of the mouth come from the heart and those defile the man." As the Scriptures reveal, Jesus was concerned with the hearts of the Pharisees—what was happening internally—but for the Pharisees, all that seemed to matter was their appearance and status.

Jesus was exposing a couple of problems. First, a person can sound really religious in their words and yet be very far from God relationally. So, while they delivered eloquent prayers, spoke using all the proper "church slang," and impressed their listeners by quoting Scripture from memory, they didn't impress God. The second issue was what was *really* going on in their hearts. While they might have been able to deceive those around them with fancy spiritual talk, they couldn't fool God, and their true character was exposed in their actions of separating themselves from the ordinary and weak.

Despite their failings, the Pharisees truly believed they were worshiping God and that they were chosen by God to carry out His work here on earth. Unfortunately, they worshiped *God's law* instead of worshiping *God*. Morality, self-discipline, and self-control became their idols, causing their hearts to turn away from God even though they proclaimed to be holy. They actually thought they were pleasing God by how "good" they were, but in reality, they were worshiping their own moral standards and their hearts were very far from God.

When we read about all of the confrontations Jesus had with the Pharisees, it's very easy for us to take Jesus' side and look upon the Pharisees with contempt. We see the Pharisees as the bad guys and conclude that we would never behave like them. Yet so many of us, particularly in the Western world, are attempting to live the Christian life through our own knowledge, ability, and effort. Ironically, this is exactly how the Pharisees lived and why Jesus had such a problem with them. They were attempting to achieve holiness on their own, completely disconnected from God. They were more concerned about their own holiness instead of loving and pursuing the Holy One. Again, they were doing all the right things for all the wrong reasons.

AMERICAN PHARISEES

Pharisees exist today but in a slightly different form. Unlike the Pharisees in Jesus' day, American Pharisees claim Jesus as Savior and Lord. They believe they are saved by grace through faith and not by keeping the law. They believe they are living the ideal Christian life because they have accepted Christ as their savior, do their best to sin less, and serve God the best they can. They read their Bibles, pray regularly, and actively participate in church functions and small groups. They financially support faith-based organizations out of a sense of duty, but they will typically give out of their excess instead of sacrificially. They tend to view kingdom building work such as missions, evangelism, and discipleship as chores and obligations that compete against busy schedules instead of recognizing these activities as privileges. They are very obedient, but their obedience is based on their own understanding of what it means to be a Christian. They base their spiritual growth on what they do instead of who they are in Christ.

In many ways, American Pharisees are similar to the Pharisees in Jesus' day because the faith they claim is with their lips while their hearts are very far from Him. These people disguise themselves as devout followers of Christ while living a very different lifestyle. It is a life that is focused more on appearances than authenticity. They are motivated by worldly success, and while they would never admit it to anyone, they secretly relish in their achievements and may even look down on others who haven't experienced worldly success or lived a virtuous life. In church settings, American Pharisees are typically unwilling to connect relationally with others. If they do attempt to connect relationally, it's only a surface connection. For instance, the person will pass by in the church hallway with a big smile, carrying a Bible. He'll wave and ask how you're doing, but he really doesn't want to know. The American Pharisee would rather assume everything is OK, because that's much less time consuming than listening to someone's problems.

They often carry a humble swagger of holy arrogance and make it clear how much they know about God. They love entering into the realm of theological debates and will fight tooth and nail to get their point across. You will find them actively serving in the church, but their serving is limited by their busy schedules and usually motivated by duty or obligation. Their demeanor can be highly admirable and respectable, causing people to look up to them, or they can be cold and offensive causing people to avoid them altogether. Still, one thing is clear about American Pharisees: they sell themselves as highly devoted for the sake of the Gospel, but internally, they are very far from God. They might sense their relational distance with God, but they don't know exactly what to do about it. So, they continue to pursue holiness and righteousness on their own terms in the hopes of drawing closer to God.

American Pharisees have been blessed with the gift of self-discipline, and they take great pride in what they do. Unfortunately, they exploit this gift for their own benefit instead of benefitting others. They use their self-discipline to gain a thorough understanding of the Scriptures, to pray, to serve, and to give. But all of these things are done with the intention of puffing themselves up or showing God how devout they are in the hopes of gaining special favor and blessing. They also want to appear holy and righteous in front of others, so they can receive praises from man and/or look down their noses at others who are unable to live up to their standards. Although most might be hesitant to admit it, they view living the Christian life as a duty or obligation, and their relationship with God tends to be distant or stale.

Before my divorce, I lived like an American Pharisee.

I thought that being a Christian was a matter of using my knowledge, ability, and effort combined with motivation, self-discipline, and focus to practice my faith. As I pursued the good life here on earth, I made sure to keep my faith at the forefront. I was always thinking to myself, what would God do in this situation? What should I do that would honor God? This mindset was emphasized with the popular WWJD (What Would Jesus Do) movement in the late 90s and early 2000s. This simple acronym allowed me to live my life by asking the rhetorical question, "What Jesus would do" in a particular situation, and then I would align my actions accordingly. I found the WWJD concept fairly easy to implement into my everyday life. If I was presented with a difficult decision, I would ask the rhetorical question, "What would Jesus Do?" Then I would seek out an answer from Scripture and allow that answer to guide my decision-making process. I viewed my Bible as "The Manual for Life" and applied it to every aspect of my daily living. While it's true that God's Word shows us how we should live, we are also unable to live the holy and righteous life He describes apart from Him. **The authentic Christian life always has and always will be a life that can only be lived in connection with Him—it is a life we live "in Christ."** It is God who is at work in the heart and soul of the believer. I made the big mistake of playing the role of Jesus by determining what I should do based on my own wisdom and understanding of Scripture, instead of allowing Jesus to transform my heart and work through me.

I also made the big mistake of using my faith as a means to obtain the desires of my heart. I preferred my desires to God's desires, and I sought after *my* kingdom of the American Dream over *God's* kingdom. Just like the Pharisees in Jesus' day, I worshipped God with my words, not with my heart. As I continued to grow in my own righteousness, I became self-righteous. Eventually, self-righteousness distorted my entire faith, yet I couldn't see it because self-righteousness does what it does best—it blinds people into thinking they are doing the right things for the right reasons.

SELF-RIGHTEOUSNESS IS SELFISHNESS

One of the most dangerous mindsets a person can have is that of self-righteousness. As the term indicates, people who are self-righteous believe that they are right in their thinking, right in their living, right in their view of religious matters. Only an act of God can grab their attention and change their heart. No amount of debate or reasoning will convince the self-righteous that they are being misled by their own thought patterns. One of the most difficult people to reach for the sake of the Gospel is the self-righteous because they don't believe they are doing anything wrong or living in opposition to God.

At the root of self-righteousness is selfishness. The self-righteous person is self-focused instead of others-focused. The pursuit of doing the right thing takes precedence over doing the kind thing. The desire to be right supersedes the desire to love others. Winning arguments become the goal rather than seeking to understand another person. Displaying a morally upright self-image is more important than being authentic and vulnerable with others.

Selfishness is in the heart of every human, and it creates barriers that prevent people from experiencing a relationship with God. Some people might naturally carry an "others" focused disposition, but even the most kind, most giving, most considerate individuals actively seek their own basic needs. Self-preservation is a

> I PREFERRED MY DESIRES TO GOD'S DESIRES, AND I SOUGHT AFTER *MY* KINGDOM OF THE AMERICAN DREAM OVER *GOD'S* KINGDOM.

natural trait found in every human being, but even self-preservation is, by definition, a selfish view of living.

Take a newborn baby, for example. All babies use self-preservation techniques to remain alive. When they are hungry or need comforted, they will cry until the parent meets the need. No loving parent would look at a crying baby and say, "Stop crying. You are just being selfish." That sort of action would be as unloving and uncaring as a parent could possibly be. Parents know that babies need basic physical requirements to survive, and they will lovingly provide those requirements and make sacrifices to ensure their children receive what they need.

Many people often seek after God out of selfish reasons. We turn to Him only after going through a hardship, loneliness, or even desiring eternal life in Heaven instead of Hell. Having selfish motives for seeking God sounds terrible, but it really just reveals the universal truth of how broken we are as human beings. God, in His infinite wisdom and perfect love, understands our brokenness and how we view things selfishly. Because He is continually pursuing us, He is free to use any means, including our own selfishness, to draw us to Himself. And just like the crying baby in need of physical food and comfort, we also cry out, so we can be fed and comforted spiritually by our Heavenly Father. God's love for us is infinitely greater than the sum of love that all parents have ever expressed to their children throughout the history of mankind. Thus, we can rest assured that

He accepts us when we turn to Him in faith. It is only by God's lovingkindness that we have an opportunity to experience a personal and intimate relationship with Him. The problem comes when we remain selfish in our ways after we have committed our lives to Christ.

For much of my Christian life prior to the divorce, I held this selfish view of what it meant to be a Christian. I now refer to this distorted view as following the "Me Gospel." It is a false view of the Gospel that promotes mankind as the end goal of the Gospel and follows these basic principles:

- God loves me and sent His Son to pay the penalty of my sins, so I can go to Heaven when I die

- While I live in this world, I will do the best I can at practicing my faith by sinning less and serving God more

- This world is broken, so I need to get through this life with as little discomfort as possible

- Therefore, I will pursue happiness, comfort, and success

- As long as I incorporate my faith into these three goals and pursue them in a morally upright and virtuous manner, I am living in God's will

- God will bless me materially if I do the best I can at being obedient to His Law and Commands

This is a convenient view of the Gospel for the independent, self-motivated, and self-disciplined American Pharisee. It provides the opportunity to experience the good life here on earth and eternal life after death. It also allows one to remain in control of one's own destiny. American Pharisees are devout followers of this way of life. The only problem is that it's not consistent with the Gospel of the Bible.

If we allow selfishness to continue to reside in our hearts after committing our lives to Christ, then we'll miss out on the greatest blessings God has to offer us—and that is the best-case scenario. The worst-case scenario is that we reap the pain, heartache, and disappointment that come from making selfish decisions. Choices that elevate, promote, and puff up one's self are always sinful because they glorify self instead of God. It's so important to realize that we are often driven by selfish motives—even when it comes to our relationship with Christ. Until we recognize this fact, our spiritual walk will be one that focuses on ourselves more than on God. John Piper once said, "We cannot view God as supremely valuable while preferring ourselves supremely."[1] Trying to follow Christ while possessing a selfish heart doesn't work because we will eventually be compelled to desire God's blessings more than God Himself. Our tendency will be to approach our relationship with Christ with the mindset of, "What has Jesus done to show His love for me" instead of the mindset, "What can I do to show my love for Him?" Love and selfishness do not mix.

GRACE ENTITLEMENT

What has caused the influx of American Pharisees in mainstream Christianity? Part of the problem is our selfish view of God's grace. Many American Pharisees view salvation as an "insurance policy" to make sure they get to Heaven. They are seeking the benefits of Christianity without making any real commitment to follow Jesus by faith. They want to receive peace, joy, forgiveness, and eternal life, but they are not willing to turn away from their old life. Some will even admit they are living sinful lives, but they respond by saying, "God will forgive me because God's grace is bigger than any sin. God is faithful, and He cannot go back on His Word." These people will claim they are saved and that they have faith, but is this a saving faith? Have they truly received God's grace, or are they claiming a promise they have yet to receive?

The faith that truly saves us from eternal separation from God is a faith that is initiated by God and given to us freely by His grace. It is not a faith we can create on our own because we can't muster up enough faith to save our souls. The justification and sanctification of salvation begins and ends with God. We are merely recipients of His favor upon us, and our faith grows as we respond to the truth of God's Word. God gives this saving grace freely, and it is a priceless gift. Once a person begins to recognize just how valuable God's grace really is, one cannot help but be changed. In the words of Charles Spurgeon, "The grace that does not change my life will not save my soul."[2]

Pride is the root issue of selfishness, and our pride is one of the greatest barriers standing in the way of the grace that changes our souls. It is not that our pride is more powerful than God's grace. Rather, we refuse His gift of grace because we desire to remain in control of our lives. We want to call the shots, so we obey God's laws when it works for us but forgo the laws and do things our way when we feel like it. When we desire to willfully and intentionally go against God, we are being deceived by our own pride. We mistakenly think we are entitled to grace, but in reality, our pride blocks us from receiving the very grace God desires to give us.

Some might question whether or not God would actually withhold His grace from someone. Actually, the

Bible makes it quite clear that He does. Romans 12:6 and Ephesians 4:7 state that we have different levels of grace given to us. More importantly, and very relevant to the topic of salvation, James 4:6 and I Peter 5:5 state that, "God opposes the proud, but gives grace to the humble." For the unbeliever, pride becomes a barrier to receiving God's saving grace. For the believer, pride becomes a barrier to experiencing the fullness of His grace. Our pride stands in opposition to God, and God will oppose those who are proud.

Paul addressed this issue of man's prideful nature in Romans. He states, "What shall we say then? Are we to continue in sin so that grace may increase? May it never be! How shall we who died to sin still live in it?" (Romans 6:1-2). Paul tells his readers that those who truly love the Lord do not continue to live carelessly in sin and take for granted the grace of God. The writer of Hebrews provides an even harsher response:

> For if we go on sinning willfully after receiving the knowledge of the truth, there no longer remains a sacrifice for sins, but a terrifying expectation of judgment and the fury of a fire which will consume the adversaries. Anyone who has set aside the Law of Moses dies without mercy on the testimony of two or three witnesses. How much more severe punishment do you think he will deserve who has trampled underfoot the Son of God, and has regarded as unclean the blood of the covenant by which he was sanctified, and has insulted the Spirit of grace? (Hebrews 10:26-28)

In other words, if you think you can live life as you please while claiming to know and love Jesus, you will face the judgment of God and *not* an eternity with Him.

God's grace provides the believer freedom *from* sin. His grace does not give the believer freedom *to* sin. To think lightly of sin is to exploit God's grace. If we desire sin, even secretly within our hearts, it is an indicator that we think less of God's grace than we care to admit. A person's view of sin says a lot about what the individual believes to be true about God, and one of the greatest sins is to refuse Christ as the Lord and Ruler of our lives. Unfortunately, our pride continually tells us that we are the rulers of our own kingdom. The degree to which we humble ourselves before God is directly tied to our understanding the value of His grace.

* * *

When I was in the midst of my divorce, I thought it was the biggest problem I'd ever encountered in my life. I was completely devastated and felt helpless and hopeless. Suffering led me to the point of questioning everything I thought I knew about God. But God, in His infinite sovereignty, used a sinful event to uncover a much bigger problem that I was completely unaware of—my own pride and self-righteousness. God allowed me to experience something I couldn't fix to show me just how inadequate and incapable I really was. He brought me to the crossroads of my faith to reveal that I had a distorted view of what it meant to be a Christian. He taught me that the Christian life is more than a one-time profession of faith followed by a life of trying to sin less and serve God more. He showed me that life doesn't always turn out okay no matter how hard I try to do all the right things. I learned that pursuing the good and nice life was competing against my pursuit of Him, and I was focused more on establishing my kingdom of the American Dream than participating in His Kingdom work. In His faithfulness to rescue me, He broke me, so He could rebuild me into the person that He'd originally designed me to be.

It is God's grace that saves us, reconciles us to Him, and grows us into the image of His likeness. Since God is the source of everything good, I no longer want Him to withhold anything good from me. I am therefore willing to humble myself under His Mighty hand (I Peter 5:6), so that I might receive His grace in increasing measure. I now realize that God's grace is not an entitlement, but rather a privilege. And His grace must be received in humility—a humility that says, "I am nothing without God, and I am more than I could ever be when I allow Him to be Lord over my life."

* * *

CHALLENGE: Begin praying on a regular basis for God to reveal any areas of self-righteousness and selfishness that exists in your life.

Questions for Reflection:

1. In what ways can you relate your faith walk to that of an American Pharisee?

2. How has this distorted view of the Gospel negatively impacted your relationship with God?

3. How has self-righteousness and selfishness caused you to misunderstand the truth about God's Word and what it means to follow Christ?

5

COMMITMENT:
THE FOUNDATION
OF RELATIONSHIP

"If anyone wishes to come after Me, he must deny himself,
and take up his cross daily and follow Me."
Luke 9:23

OCTOBER 2010

*M*eredith was at school, and I was working from
home. As I sat in the great room, I paused to take
a look around the house. While all of the furniture,
pictures, and decor remained unchanged, so much had changed
between Alyson and me. The house felt so empty and bare. All
of our family memories were locked away in photo albums
and hidden in the recesses of my mind—they almost seemed
like figments of my imagination. The sorrow that invaded
my heart was unbearable; I dared not look into the albums or
ponder the memories for fear that I might recall a moment that
I desperately wanted to experience once again. Not only was
our home emptied of past memories, but it was devoid of all

future dreams—this was the last day that Alyson and I would be husband and wife. Now that she was living in an apartment, her physical presence was no longer a part of our home, and there I was, sitting in my chair, holding shattered memories and broken dreams, unable to escape the reality that she was gone. The emptiness of our good and nice home seemed to scream at me. Its loud silence reminded me of its transformation from a dream home to a shell of a house.

About midmorning, I heard a knock on the door. It was Alyson. Since our court hearing was the following day, I had asked her to come over in one last attempt to persuade her not to go through with the divorce. I wasn't even sure if she would show up, so I was surprised when she arrived. Since the day she told me that she wanted to leave, I'd been praying that she'd have a change of heart. The fact that she came over at all gave me a glimmer of hope, and I was confident that God could work a miracle if He chose.

It had been a little over a month since she'd moved out, and as I watched her slowly make her way to the kitchen table, I saw her looking around our home. I wondered if she was also experiencing the sorrow of dead memories and dreams. As we both sat at the table where we'd shared so many meals together, I held her hand and tenderly pleaded, "It's not too late. I know that our court date is tomorrow, but you have the power to stop this. We can start over again—just like we did when we first met. It will take a lot of work from both of us, but if you are willing, I know we can overcome this fracture in our marriage."

She didn't respond right away. I waited for her to say something. Then with teary eyes, she said, "I feel like the glass has shattered into a million pieces, and I don't know how to put everything back together again."

I didn't know what to say; all I knew was that I didn't want our marriage to end. We both sat in silence for what felt like an eternity, and then I replied, "We both owe it to Meredith to give it a shot. Let's take it step by step, and we'll figure it out." After another painfully long stretch of silence, she simply said, "I need to go." She quietly left her chair and walked out of our home for the last time as my wife. I then sat in what would become my house, trying to put together the pieces of my life that had been shattered. The commitment we'd made on that beautiful day in May of 1998 would officially be nullified just a little over twenty-four hours later.

* * *

THE DIVINE DESIGN OF MARRIAGE

While every relationship requires commitment to thrive, marriage is the strongest, most intimate commitment of any human relationship. Marriage was designed by God as a lifelong covenant between one man and one woman, where two become one flesh (Genesis 2:18-24). In marriage, both man and woman make a commitment to hold the relationship higher than themselves. Each one puts away selfish ambition and personal desires by making selfless sacrifices for the relationship to grow and strengthen. With this proper perspective of commitment, the relationship thrives as the two pursue each other. The blessing that comes from this pursuit and sacrifice can only be experienced within the confines of the marriage covenant. It is a lifelong commitment that becomes stronger and more fulfilling than any other human relationship on earth.

It's important to recognize that God didn't design marriage as an arbitrary afterthought. He intentionally created marriage to be a relationship that reflects Christ's relationship with the Church (Ephesians 5:22-33). Through marriage, we gain a better understanding of the closeness and intimacy that each one of us can experience with Christ. Still, marriage is only a reflection of our relationship with Christ, as our personal connection with Christ is designed to be so much closer and more intimate than marriage. Unfortunately, ever since the fall of man, marriage has been under attack by the enemy to distort our view of what marriage is supposed to represent. As a result, even at its very best, marriage is hard work and requires a tremendous amount of sacrifice in order to thrive.

TWO TYPES OF COMMITMENT: NEEDS-SEEKING VERSUS SACRIFICIAL-GIVING

The very foundation of every marriage is commitment, and a marriage will only be as strong as the least committed individual. Marriage is both a one-time profession of this commitment on the wedding day and then a lifelong commitment that grows stronger thereafter because of the couple's desire to know each other relationally. They pursue each other, not out of obligation or compliance to their marriage license, but rather out of devotion and affection. As they pursue each other, they give sacrificially by letting go of their own personal preferences for the sake of demonstrating their love. Day after day, year after year, this **sacrificial-giving** strengthens the commitment more and more. Clearly, the strength of commitment is directly related to the degree to which the couple is willing to sacrifice for each other.

Unfortunately, our American culture does not view commitment from this sacrificial-giving standpoint, but rather from a **needs-seeking** point of view. The main goal of this secular approach to marriage is to determine if the other person will meet one's needs. They approach marriage on a trial and error basis in order to "make sure" the other person is Mr. or Mrs. Right. In other words, a couple will try to determine if it's a good marital match by obtaining the benefits of marriage without actually being married. They follow the misguided idea that they can test marriage out by pretending to be married, believing that proceeding with caution is the best approach. If it doesn't work, one or both can decide to walk away before ever truly getting married.

This needs-seeking approach to marriage sets the wedding day as the end goal. As the dating relationship grows, the couple will test their compatibility by having sex. If the sex is great, then they will move on to the next stage of compatibility—living together. If living together works out, then they will proceed to marriage. Throughout this process, they believe they are "playing it safe" by testing the waters for compatibility. The couple incorrectly thinks they are committed to each other at each phase of the relationship because they keep proceeding to the next phase of intimacy. However, the entire relationship is based on a false sense of commitment because one or both is working under the assumption that if things don't work out, someone can always decide to leave. Thus, no real commitment can be found in this type of arrangement because one or both individuals is so focused on having individual needs met that the two most important questions about marriage that *should* be asked are *never* asked. Those questions are as follows: Am I willing to sacrificially give myself to this person unconditionally for the rest of my life? Has this person consistently demonstrated a willingness to sacrificially give to me unconditionally?

The couple's false sense of commitment is based on each person's needs being met by the other and does not represent the true selfless commitment that God originally designed for marriage. This modern-day American view of marriage is one in which the wedding day becomes the destination instead of the starting point for an authentic lifelong commitment. The couple attempts to "play married" by pursuing cohabitation over commitment. They want all of the benefits of marriage without putting forth the true commitment that is required. Once the couple reaches the pinnacle of achievement by making it to the wedding day, they continue to approach marriage from a self-centered view, where individual preferences take precedence over one's spouse. In this context, commitment becomes conditional to one's needs being met. As long as the person feels loved and one's needs are being met, then that person is committed to the marriage. However, if they don't feel loved or their needs are not being met, then they begin to wonder if something better is out there, and commitment takes second place to self-fulfillment.

THE PROBLEMS OF A CONTRIVED COMMITMENT

The problem with the modern-day approach to marriage is twofold. First, the foundation of marriage has been established on a false view of commitment. The unspoken agreement between the couple prior to the wedding day is that either one can walk away at any time if personal needs are not being met. The underlying assumption is, "As long as I'm happy, I will stay." This is not representative of the true selfless commitment required for marriage. Whether they intend it or not, this needs-seeking view of commitment continues to be the foundation of the entire relationship, resulting in an exponentially higher risk for an unsatisfactory marriage and higher risk of divorce.

Secondly, the couple is working under the false assumption that married life can be simulated outside of marriage. No matter how hard a couple tries, it is simply impossible to create an environment that represents marriage without actually being married. Regardless of how long the couple decides to live together, neither one has taken that sacrificial step into the lifelong commitment of marriage. Interestingly, most people know intuitively that marriage will change a couple, which is precisely why people choose to cohabitate before getting married. If the couple were truly committed to each other, they would get married instead of attempting to simulate marriage. However, they prefer to do a trial run of cohabitation under the false belief that they can figure out if they are truly committed. But just as a person cannot be half born, half pregnant, or half dead, a person cannot be half committed to marriage. They are either committed or not, and living together before marriage will not answer the commitment question.

Unfortunately, many people who profess faith in Christ have adopted this cultural view of marriage. It is disheartening to see the number of people in Christian circles who believe that having sex and living together before getting married is not only harmless but even encouraged. They do not ask themselves, "Am I willing to give myself to this person for the rest of my life to develop a relationship that is more important than my own personal needs or desires?" Instead, they fool themselves by thinking, "I really need to figure out if this person is the right one to meet all of my needs." Approaching marriage from a needs-seeking perspective can create significant damage even if the couple does not end up divorced, and this approach can damage other relationships as well.

OUR COMMITMENT TO CHRIST: DEEP OR SHALLOW WATERS?

The term "accepting Christ" is popular in mainstream Christianity. Anyone who has attended an evangelical church for any length of time has probably heard this term used to describe people who have committed their lives to Christ. Unfortunately, in many churches across America, the term "accepting Christ" has watered down the commitment believers have to Christ. The term "accepting Christ" misleads people when they begin to believe that to become a Christian all one needs is a one-time profession of faith followed by baptism. Thus, "accepting Christ" is viewed as the destination—we just want them to "accept Christ." By making this one-time event the focus, instead of the starting point to a life-long relationship with God, the salvation message is watered down, and the general message of this watered-down view of salvation is this:

> God loves you and has a wonderful plan for your life. He desperately wants a relationship with you. All you have to do is accept Jesus in your heart and you will be saved. Just say this prayer: "Dear God, I know I'm a sinner, and I ask for your forgiveness. I believe Jesus Christ is Your Son. I believe that He died for my sins and that you raised Him to life. I want to trust Him as my Savior and Lord. I pray all of this in the name of Jesus. Amen." That's it. That's all you need to do. You are now born again and will receive eternal life.

While all of the elements within the above statements are true, the "sinner's prayer" does not provide a full picture of what it means to make a life-long commitment to following Christ by truly claiming Him as Lord.

Many people have been attracted to the watered-down version of the salvation message because it's one where they can "get saved" and then continue living their lives as they please, regardless of how sinful or how virtuous they are. Similar to the modern-day American view of marriage, their relationship with Christ is based on trans-actional terms—they will remain conditionally committed to God as long as He blesses them with what they want. Again, we see the needs-seeking commitment rear its ugly head because this needs-seeking type of love prevents the relationship from thriving. As in the skewed view of marriage, it is a type of commitment to God that implies, "As long as my needs are met and I can fit my faith into my hectic schedule, I'm in. Otherwise, I'm just focusing on my day to day living."

While many believers would be reluctant to admit they prescribe to this belief, their behaviors exhibit what they truly believe. Most professed believers in Jesus are committed only up to a point—that point is when their commitment begins to cost them to give up something they desire. So, they are comfortable in serving but *only* if it fits into their busy agendas. They will give money *as long* as it doesn't interfere with their own material desires or financial goals. They will read their Bibles and pray, but only when searching for an answer or helping with a situation. They only want enough of Christ to pull them through a hardship or help them achieve ambitious goals. They view Jesus as a college intern who helps them navigate through life instead of the CEO of their life.

TRUE COMMITMENT TO CHRIST

The Bible is very clear that repentance and faith are required for salvation. That is to say, a person is saved when one truly believes every element within the sinner's prayer to personally be true. This belief is more than just an intellectual acknowledgement that we are saved by grace through faith—it's a belief that is acted upon from that moment forward. Saving faith means we *declare* and *live* as though Jesus is the ruler of our lives. Thus, as we walk through life, we follow Him instead of following our own plans. It is a life committed to sacrificial-giving.

So what do true belief and commitment to Christ look like? Here are Charles Spurgeon's thoughts on the matter:

> What does it mean to believe in Him? It is not merely to say, "He is God and the Savior," but to trust Him wholly and entirely, and take Him for all your salvation from this time forth and forever—your Lord, your Master, your all. If you will have Jesus, He has you already. If you believe on Him, you cannot go to hell; for that would make the sacrifice of Christ of none effect.[3]

The true believer trusts Jesus to be Lord of one's life. Jesus Himself discussed the amount of sacrifice involved in the Christian life when He said, "If anyone wishes to come after Me, he must deny himself, and take up his cross daily and follow Me" (Luke 9:23). As Jesus revealed, believing Jesus is a daily commitment to follow Him and trust Him with our lives. In doing so, we have the opportunity to experience Him and grow in our relationship with Him.

How Do We Learn Sacrifice?

Because humans are naturally sinful, the question arises: how do we love the Lord, our spouses, and others in a sacrificial way? Thankfully, God doesn't expect us to figure out how to live as a sacrificial giver on our own. If you're a believer, He equips you to do so by making you a new creation. One of my favorite illustrations in Scripture of our new birth is where Paul states, "Therefore if anyone is in Christ, he is a new creature; the old things passed away; behold new things have come. Now all these things are from God, who reconciled us to Himself through Christ and gave us the ministry of reconciliation" (II Corinthians. 5:17-18). As Paul reveals, God's grace has given us the opportunity to be a **new creation**. So, our faith is more than just a feeling or trusting—it is action-based and results in a new life for the believer.

Jesus, Himself, discussed this new life of the believer when He said, "Truly, truly, I say to you, unless one is born again, he cannot see the kingdom of God" (John 3:3). Just as we cannot make ourselves be born physically, we also cannot make ourselves be born spiritually. Both physical and spiritual birth must be initiated by someone else. And the Scriptures are clear: when it comes to our spiritual birth, it is God who initiates. He gives us a new heart—one that has been changed from a heart of stone to a heart of flesh. He has made us new.

Another way to think of the new creation is by examining what has happened to our previous selves. In Romans, Paul shed light on the new life of the believer by discussing the death of our old self:

> Our old self was crucified with Him, in order that our body of sin might be done away with, so that we

would no longer be slaves to sin, for he who has died is freed from sin. (Romans 6:6-7)

As Paul revealed, our old, sinful self was put to death so that our old ways might be done away with. Remember, it is God who makes us this new creation, so if our primary focus as a Christian is behavior modification and self-discipline, then we haven't yet died to ourselves and allowed Christ to take over our lives.

Along with the death of our old selves comes repentance or a turning away from our old life. However, repentance is not a work that we must do to receive salvation, but rather, repentance is found within our saving faith. It's when we turn to God and allow Him to change us, instead of trying to change ourselves. If we are saved by God's grace, we will turn away from our old life and turn to Christ. This sacrificial-giving type of commitment is a product of salvation alone. We are saved by grace through faith, and that saving faith is evidenced by our desire to turn our lives over to Him in true commitment. We give up our throne and make Him the ruler of our lives.

WE ARE A LIVING SACRIFICE

The key to moving away from a needs-seeking view of commitment is sacrifice. When we make sacrifices for a relationship, we give up something we perceive as valuable to make the relationship stronger. And, as the relationship grows stronger, the relationship becomes more valuable. By willingly giving up personal preferences for the sake of growing the relationship, we demonstrate to the other person that we are committed to them, rather than to ourselves.

In general, the word sacrifice does not bring up pleasurable thoughts. We tend to think of sacrifice in terms of loss or having to give something up. But another way to think of sacrifice is in terms of planned suffering. Even though we are giving something up, we are actually receiving something much better in return. We are not sacrificing with the hope of winning the favor of another person—that would actually be an unhealthy relationship. We *choose* to sacrifice, recognizing that our personal preferences are less desirable than the relationship.

When we think about our relationship with God, we can be assured that any sacrifice will be met, in turn, with something way more fulfilling. As Christians, we have been given the ability to shed the desires of our old selves because they hinder us from experiencing God's best, and when we begin to see just how awesome our God is, we will begin preferring Him to our desires. As a result, we will want to join Him in His kingdom work here on earth by reflecting His love to everyone around us, and we'll begin giving up our personal pursuits and ambitions to join in His work. As we go through this process of shedding old desires, we connect more closely with God and discover the sacrifice is not for God's benefit—it is for our own benefit.

Unfortunately, American Pharisees will generally not consider suffering for the sake of Christ because they have bought into the "Me Gospel" and view their commitment to Christ from a needs-seeking perspective. I believe this is one of the primary reasons the modern-day church is filled with people who claim a faith but do little to nothing in terms of the Great Commission. Sadly, the American culture of consumerism has crept into their faith and their view of relationships. Thus, the American Pharisee uses faith as a type of currency in order to receive something from God, and relationships as a type of currency to receive something from others. They are unable to view faith and relationships from a sacrificial-giving perspective, which contrasts the Bible's view that suffering for Christ is integral to being a Christian: "For I consider that the sufferings of this present time are not worthy to be compared with the glory that is to be revealed to us" (Romans 8:18). In fact, this is how we know we are committed to Christ—when we are willing to sacrificially suffer in His name for His glory.

* * *

How we think about our spouse and how we view marriage reveal our true opinions about God. As I think back on my marriage with Alyson, my biggest shortfall was that my commitment to her was needs-seeking. This selfish commitment began when we decided to live together before we were married. I knew living together before marriage was wrong; no one needed to remind me. Unfortunately, I allowed the popular worldview to influence me to the point that I consciously chose the wrong decision and justified my choice by claiming it made financial sense. My "logic" was as follows: Both Alyson and I were coming to the end of our leases and were already engaged, so we figured, why not just move into one apartment? After all, we were committed to one another—or so I thought. We could cut our monthly rent in half and pick an apartment that would work for us once we got married. I truly believe this one wrong decision set the entire course of our marriage down the wrong path.

This choice reveals a lot about who I was at that time in my life. It takes a real idiot to say, "I know this decision is wrong, but I'm going to do it anyway." Unfortunately, that is precisely what I did. Even more, I rationalized my terrible decision by claiming it made logical sense from a financial standpoint. If I had been sacrificially committed to Alyson, then I would have looked out for her best interests and taken a stand for what I knew was best for our future. As the leader, I should have required us to get married first. But instead, I chose personal convenience, personal desire, and personal finances over the wise decision. It's amazing and frightening the lengths a person will go to rationalize sinful behavior.

Not surprisingly, my selfish view of commitment continued into our marriage. I found myself focusing on my career and success more than I focused on pursuing Alyson. I wanted to live the American Dream. Even though my worldly pursuits were morally upright and noble, I began preferring the good and nice life to my relationship with

> HOW WE THINK ABOUT OUR SPOUSE AND HOW WE VIEW MARRIAGE REVEAL OUR TRUE OPINIONS ABOUT GOD.

Alyson. My desire to achieve the American Dream was a type of idolatry against my marriage.

Eventually, Alyson and I began living parallel lives, and I'm convinced that our destiny of parallel living began when we chose to live together before getting married. We viewed our marriage as the destination instead of the starting point. We celebrated the victory on our wedding day, but not long after, we began our slow fade into complacency because our commitment was founded upon our own needs being met instead of meeting each other's needs.

In addition, my broken marriage revealed that I also had a selfish commitment to God. I preferred the "good life" to the "God-life." The American Dream became my idol, and I began worshiping America's holy trinity—happiness, comfort, and success. I gave God much of my life, but not sacrificially. I only gave until it began to interfere with the life I wanted. I was living the American Pharisee lifestyle to the fullest. I pursued the "Me Gospel" and believed that as long as I stayed in God's good graces by reading my Bible, praying, and serving, then God would continue to bless me. Selfishly, I wanted God's blessing more than I wanted God Himself. I failed to recognize that a person who is truly committed to Christ gives sacrificially through humility, surrender, and obedience.

True love is sacrificial, and sacrifice values another over personal preferences. In real sacrifice, I give up something I desire without any expectation of receiving in return. The Apostles understood this and were willing to endure great suffering. They were committed.

Are you committed?

Are you willing to suffer for no other reason than to be identified as a Christ-follower?

Are you willing to give up the easy life in exchange for an abundant life?

What has your faith cost you?

If you are married and recognize you're in a needs-seeking commitment to your spouse, there is a high probability you're also in a needs-seeking commitment to Christ. A needs-seeking commitment does not and cannot work because it's a conditional commitment—and that's just another term for being uncommitted.

COMMITMENT

* * *

CHALLENGE: Consider if you approach commitments from a needs-seeking perspective or a sacrificial-giving perspective.

Questions for Reflection:

If you profess to be a Christ-follower, think back to the moment you made that personal decision.

1. What was your motive for coming to Christ?

2. Was your motive a selfish one?

3. If your salvation experience was driven by a selfish motive, has your faith moved from the mindset that says, "What has Jesus done to show His love for me?" to the mindset of, "What can I do for Jesus to show my love for Him?" If not, what is preventing you from making this transition?

If you have not yet made the lifelong commitment of following Christ, take a moment to strongly consider what is preventing you from making this decision. Now is the time to make that commitment.

6

HUMILITY:
FINDING STRENGTH

"For who regards you as superior? What do you have that you did not receive? And if you did receive it, why do you boast as if you had not received it?" I Corinthians 4:7

NOVEMBER 2010

*T*he humiliation of divorce had been setting in for several weeks. I was unable to keep my marriage together, and everyone knew it. All of the years of success and achievement had been nullified by this one event. Ironically, I viewed my marriage as the most secure aspect of my American Dream. While I believed that I couldn't count on anything else in this world, I thought I could at least count on my wife to be with me for better or for worse. But the one person I relied on the most had betrayed me. Because I couldn't keep my marriage together, I felt like a complete failure—and I wasn't familiar with failing. I was in uncharted waters and completely out of my comfort zone. Worst of all, being viewed as a divorced man humiliated me.

The biggest source of my shame actually came from those who were fellow Christians. I'll never forget a conversation I had with a distant cousin on my dad's side of the family. Only because she'd asked, I shared with her my story of divorce. I was transparent and poured my heart out to her. I told her how much I didn't want the divorce, how I did everything I could to keep the marriage together, but in the end, my marriage ended. I also shared how I felt God's presence in the midst of my suffering and was so thankful for my faith and all that I was learning about God's character. After sharing my deepest wound with her, she replied, "Our God is full of grace. He will surely forgive you of your divorce." Her statement seemed to completely ignore the pain of my experience, and it seemed more important to her to make sure I was aware of my sin. Instead of giving compassion to someone who'd been betrayed by a spouse, she preferred to beat me down even further with truth and righteousness. I'm sure that from her perspective she thought she was helping me better understand God's grace. But in reality, she didn't offer me anything of real value. I already knew about the sinfulness of divorce and God's grace to forgive. I didn't need anyone to remind me of these spiritual truths while I was in the midst of suffering. What I really needed was empathy and compassion. I was so shocked by her response that I didn't even know what to say, so I just sheepishly smiled and said, "Thanks," before walking away. Sometimes, those who claim a faith can be some of the harshest and most judgmental people on earth. Sadly, they don't even realize it. Their pride is disguised as humble arrogance, and this false sense of humility causes them to be trapped in a pit of self-righteousness. Truth absent of love is nothing but cruelty.

Even more, there were some people at church who made me feel like an outcast. Clearly from their perspective, I was the guy who must have done something wrong to deserve divorce. While most of these people didn't say anything directly to me, they didn't have to. They just stopped talking to me and looked the other way. Apparently, I was being shunned for committing the sin of divorce. It was almost as if I was carrying a disease, and they were afraid it was contagious.

Still, I am eternally grateful for the pastoral staff and those few close friends at church who truly loved me and stood by my side. Without their representing Christ's love to me, I probably would've become jaded with church altogether. I'm so thankful for the ones who supported me through my divorce. They cared for me and were genuinely concerned for my well-being. They demonstrated true Christian love by helping me and not expecting anything in return even though some fellow believers made me feel extremely uncomfortable and even unwelcome.

In hindsight, I can't really blame my distant cousin or those fellow believers for treating me as a second-class Christian. I don't hold anything against them because I once walked in their shoes. I used to put on my Sunday morning façade every week as I pretended I had it all together and knew all the right answers for living the Christian life. I always assumed that anyone who was going through a divorce deserved it because they must have messed up somewhere along the way. Until I experienced divorce myself, I never realized the truth that it takes two to get married, but only one to get a divorce. It's interesting how we begin to see things differently through the lens of humility.

* * *

Both humility and pride are directly related to how we see ourselves and how we think about others, but these attitudes are on opposite ends of the spectrum. Pride can simply be defined as putting self before others. It's the attitude of holding a higher opinion of ourselves than we ought to hold and/or holding a lower opinion of others. The result of this attitude plays out in either direct or indirect rudeness and disrespect towards others. It is a type of selfishness that says, "I'm really not interested in you, and I don't care about you." On the other hand, humility is in direct contrast to pride. It is putting others before self, and true humility understands who we are in relation to Christ. With humility, we can view others as more important than ourselves without losing our identity. As such, we display courtesy and respect by caring more for another person's interests and well-being than our own. It is a type of sacrifice that says, "I'm truly interested in you and want the best for you." It's impossible to be humble and prideful at the same time. We are either expressing an attitude of humility or pride in any given situation.

THE COMPARISON APPROACH: HOW PRIDE SURFACES

Do I view others as more important than me? Am I courteous and respectful to others? Am I more concerned for the well-being of others than I am for myself? Most believers will intuitively answer, "yes" to these questions without giving much further thought. And the reason why most people will answer, "yes" is because people naturally think more highly of themselves than they ought. Ironically, our pride allows us to set the standard of humility, and then we judge others according to the very standard we have established.

The pride within gives us laser focus in identifying prideful behavior in other people. One of the most distasteful expressions of pride is pride masquerading as humility. For example, American Pharisees believe they are promoting humility when they chastise the entitled. They make statements such as, "Those people are so entitled. Why don't they use their affluence and influence to help others instead of wasting their resources on themselves?" They condemn the privileged, and in doing so, they believe they are humble. They become the humility police and issue tickets to those who show a higher opinion of themselves than they should. Ironically, it is the pride of the American Pharisee that condemns the privileged.

Pride can also be found in our motives for serving those who are less fortunate. American Pharisees serve the poor in an attempt to rescue them from whatever it is they are lacking. Instead of treating them like human beings, American Pharisees treat them like projects. They convince themselves that they are serving the less fortunate, but their motives are driven by a desire to fix them. They are misled into thinking *they* are the savior, and they arrive at the scene to deliver the needy from their hardship. Providing material needs, emotional support, or spiritual guidance while lacking real love for humanity is rooted in self-righteousness, not humility.

When we rely on our own efforts to solve the problems of those who have less than us while simultaneously condemning those who possess more than us, we have merely created a type of man-made humility. In reality, we are attempting to cover up our own pride by disguising it as humility. Our pride deceives us into thinking we're humble when we condemn the proud and fix the broken on our own terms.

HUMBLE ARROGANCE

Even though believers may quietly acknowledge that humility is an admirable trait, society at large views humility as weakness. In fact, humility is often perceived as a barrier to achieving excellence and greatness. Listen to almost any motivational speaker, and you won't hear humility mentioned very often. You certainly will not hear that humility is the key to strength and power. If anyone is to get ahead in life, then they need to have self-confidence, courage, determination, self-discipline, and motivation. Our American culture is bombarded with platitudes filling our heads with the secrets to success. Some of these cliché sayings include:

- Be proud of who you are

- Believe in yourself

- You are enough

- You can do anything you set your mind to

- Never change who you are

Inspirational statements such as these make us feel good about ourselves—perhaps just a little bit too good. They build us up and equip us with the courage we need to conquer anything the world throws at us. But is the cost of such courage an inflation of our own egos? Our American culture reassures us that a sense of pride is socially acceptable, and we are encouraged to dream big in order to achieve big. This worldly wisdom captures our attention like shiny red apples pleasing to the eye.

If we take these statements and allow them to guide us through life here on earth, it won't take long before we rely on our own self-sufficiency to succeed in this world. We begin deceiving ourselves into thinking we accomplished, we achieved, we conquered. In an effort to appear humble, we may give God the credit for a successful career, beautiful house, fancy car, and nice clothes. However, within our hearts, where no one else can see, we whisper, "Well done. You deserve all of the benefits for working so hard. You earned it!" Just because we bury our pride within us doesn't mean it doesn't exist. We may become very good at convincing others and ourselves we are humble, but in the end, it's really just humble arrogance disguised as pride.

American Pharisees display humble arrogance when it comes to practicing their faith. They rely on their own knowledge to understand the Bible, on their own self-discipline to pray, on their own effort to serve, and on their own motivation to give. Many appear very successful at practicing the Christian disciplines. But if they were honest with themselves, they would say their spiritual life is stale and boring. They experience a God who is distant, cold, and impersonal. But it's no wonder—they are attempting to live out their faith independently from their Creator. Whether incidentally or intentionally, they are attempting to be self-sufficient Christians. They are taking the highly valued principles of this world—such as independence, discipline, motivation, and education—and using them to grow their faith on their own terms instead of abiding in Christ and allowing the Holy Spirit to transform their lives.

In reality, there is no such thing as a self-sufficient Christian, because all things originate from God and are given to us. This is a difficult concept for most first-world Christians to understand because they are convinced that self-sufficiency is not only good, but it is also the answer to all of life's problems—including their faith. Independence may be highly valued in America, but it was never intended to be the way of life in God's Kingdom. We were created to be fully dependent upon God; living otherwise is intentionally rebelling against God's design. Recognizing our complete dependency on God is the starting point of experiencing a humble heart. As we grow in awareness of our dependency on God, our humility will also grow.

If left unchecked, self-sufficiency will eventually transition to self-righteousness. American Pharisees begin to view the Christian faith as a lifelong pursuit of behavior modification as they try to become the best version of themselves according to the standards set forth in the Bible. Their mindset of self-sufficiency leads them to the false conclusion that they can live a righteous life through their own discipline, motivation, and effort. And the more they rely on themselves to practice the Christian disciplines, the more confident they become in their own abilities. This confidence reflects a type of man-made holiness that eventually creates barriers with other believers and repels non-believers. Their pride is disguised as righteousness, but it is not the true righteousness of God that they are displaying. It is a self-righteousness obtained on their own.

> INDEPENDENCE MAY BE HIGHLY VALUED IN AMERICA, BUT IT WAS NEVER INTENDED TO BE THE WAY OF LIFE IN GOD'S KINGDOM.

CONFESSIONS OF AN AMERICAN PHARISEE

In my days of living as an American Pharisee, I was completely blind to my self-righteousness simply because I thought I was "right." Instead of allowing God's righteousness to transform my heart and produce the good works He established from the beginning, I relied on my own good deeds to be a reflection of my righteousness. Virtually anyone is capable of doing a good deed if they focus on the virtue of the act. But only Christ followers are capable of what God considers to be a good work. Still, a believer can become misled by focusing on the good deeds themselves instead of allowing the Holy Spirit to produce good works within them.

As an American Pharisee, I used my faith as a moral compass to guide me toward a type of righteousness that honored God's laws and did not hurt others. Using the golden rule as the litmus test, I relied on my own discernment to determine if my actions were appropriate. As long as I held myself accountable to consistently applying the church disciplines, then I believed I could pursue the good life as long as it stayed within the moral and ethical boundaries of God's commands. I desired to be a living testimony that worldly success, high moral ideals, and the Christian faith were not mutually exclusive. All three could be experienced simultaneously without having to sacrifice one to obtain another.

EXAMINING HOW A PHARISEE EXECUTES THE CHURCH DISCIPLINES

Reading the Scriptures: Shortly after I graduated college, I became very disciplined at reading my Bible. I would study it like a textbook as I recognized it as the authority on all philosophical matters. I was fascinated with theological topics such as original sin, assurance of salvation, is Christ the only way to God, what happens to those who don't hear the Gospel, and Calvinism versus Armenianism. I loved the intellectual challenge it brought, and I learned a tremendous amount of Biblical knowledge.

While this approach educated me about doctrine and theology, it didn't offer the closeness and intimacy with God that my soul was craving. What was worse is that I began to believe I could figure out the answer to any theological question. I became confident in my knowledge, and I was ready to debate the sharpest philosophers, whether they were Buddhists, Muslims, Hindus, or Atheists. I wanted to prove that my God was the true God, and Christ was the only way to receive eternal life with God. In my arrogance, I completely lost sight of the fact that these debates were self-serving and weren't going to change the opinions of the people I was debating. I also ignored the fact that the best-laid argument for the Christian faith is completely worthless unless God is involved in changing the person's heart. Even worse, I began drawing my own conclusions on spiritual matters instead of trusting God to reveal Himself through the Scriptures. I continued this academic approach to studying the Bible and believed all I needed was to just "figure it out" using my own knowledge, ability, and effort. I approached the Bible as a textbook and read it using my own intellect instead of relying on God's revelation to give me answers.

Praying: Throughout most of my adulthood, I prayed regularly, but my prayer life remained fairly shallow. Even though I became more sophisticated at asking for things or confessing sin, in terms of real spiritual maturity, there was very little growth in my prayer life. Honestly, if I were to break down my prayers, it would look something like the following:

Personal requests: 50% of my prayer time
Confessing sin: 35% of my prayer time
Praying for others: 10% of my prayer time
Giving thanks to God: 4% of my prayer time
Being in awe and wonder of God and silent in His presence: Less than 1%

When I look back on my motives for confessing sin, praying for others, and giving thanks to God, all of it was usually done out of selfish motives. Certainly, there were times when I experienced true authentic prayer and a connection with God. But for the majority of time, my prayers were tainted with the hidden motive of wanting God to bless me in some way or save me from some type of unfortunate circumstance. I rarely asked God what He was trying to teach me. Looking back, I can't believe how ridiculous I was to think I could hide my ulterior motive from God when He already knows my every thought.

Obeying the Commandments: My desire to obey the commandments led me to view God's Word as my rule-book for life. In a sense, the Bible is our rulebook on life, but that is only of secondary importance. I lost sight of the Bible's primary purpose—in it God reveals Himself to mankind and His plan to redeem the world. Sure, the Bible provides us with all of the rules for living a holy life, but this holy life cannot be obtained by obeying God's law. Holy living can only come from a person—Jesus Christ. Without Christ, the commandments can only condemn. With Christ, the commandments are written upon our hearts and become a reflection of God's character in our lives.

Since I knew that I was saved by grace, I never thought of myself as a "performance-based" Christian. While I believed there wasn't any amount of good deeds that could earn my salvation, I secretly thought that following God's rules would keep me in God's good graces. I naturally assumed He would bless me if I worked hard at following His rules. My distorted view of this performance-based blessing came from my desire of wanting to live "the good life" more than wanting to live for God. I was more interested in God's blessing than God Himself.

Actively Serving in Church: Going to church every Sunday wasn't even a question. It was so ingrained into my life that I never even considered casual involvement in church, and I will be forever grateful for my parents' modeling this way of life. Unfortunately, I began using my involvement as a barometer of my righteousness. Even though I was actively involved at church and served in many roles, my driving motive was a sense of obligation and duty. Rarely did I see serving as a privilege, an honor, and an opportunity to magnify God.

I also served on the condition that it must fit into my busy schedule. As I was so exhausted from the demands from work, I didn't have much left in me to serve well. I became burned out from serving, and I failed to see that my burnout was a symptom of a much bigger problem—I was relying on my own ability and effort to serve instead of allowing God to work in me. I prioritized serving over spiritual growth, and I wrongly assumed that my wages of serving would result in material blessings.

After meeting the demands from my career and serving, I didn't have much energy left over for my family—Alyson and Meredith just got the leftovers. I rationalized that it was the sacrifice all of us had to make in order to live an upper-class lifestyle and be blessed materially. I would tell everyone with a sense of pride that my priorities in life were God, family, others, and then career. But the time and effort I dedicated to each of these areas of my life was completely inverted. My words said one thing, while my actions demonstrated something completely different.

Giving: For American Pharisees, Malachi 3:10 is a favorite Scripture as it states that God will pour out His blessing to those who give back the first 10% of everything they've received. Will God bless people materially? Sure. As a matter of fact, there are many Scriptures where God blesses His children materially. However, God did not call us to be rich; He called us to be faithful to Him. And my prosperity led me to prefer material blessings over God Himself.

I now recognize that the prosperity gospel is inconsistent with what the Bible teaches, but this false gospel worked well for me during my years of pursuing a prosperous career. It fit my lifestyle and my goals, so I incorporated it into my faith. Rationalizing Scripture and theology to fit into a certain lifestyle is a dangerous proposition and the predecessor to heresy. In hindsight, this is extremely terrifying because I didn't even realize I was doing it. I simply read the Scriptures related to material blessing and claimed those Scriptures as true for me. I conveniently forgot that it is God who determines whom He will bless materially, not me. This is how I used tithing as a means to pursue the curse of affluence. I became so disciplined in tithing that it became a habit, which also became a problem. My giving became second nature, but I only gave out of my abundance instead of giving sacrificially. I never really challenged myself to give more than 10%, nor did I give it "cheerfully" as the Bible describes we should give. I simply tithed out of duty and with an expectation that God would continue to bless me financially.

Sharing the Gospel: I viewed my career as an opportunity to honor Christ by promoting Christian principles in corporate America and also conducted myself as a model employee. But over a period of time, I began to recognize that the "St. Francis strategy" wasn't very effective for me. Rarely did anyone ever ask me why I was such a stand-up guy. Many people gave me compliments regarding my work ethic and integrity, but they never really asked why I possessed these talents. Additionally, I knew many unbelievers in the office who also demonstrated the same virtuous attributes that I displayed. I certainly saw the importance for Christians to live morally upright lives; otherwise, I'd be a hypocrite. However, actions alone do not help others come to the knowledge of God. In my silent witness, I failed to realize the truth that faith comes from hearing God's Word (Romans 10:17), not from watching another person's actions. Nevertheless, I continued to utilize the "St. Francis strategy" throughout my career because it was comfortable and safe. As a result, I was often left discouraged that my witnessing efforts weren't very fruitful.

Needless to say, I wasn't very effective in sharing my faith with others, and I didn't have much desire to share. I was too busy with my career and practicing the Christian disciplines, so I didn't have much time or energy to share my faith. When I tried to share my faith, I acted less like a witness and more like an attorney. Instead of sharing what I have seen and heard, I tried to defend the Christian faith. I failed to meet people where they were and understand where they were coming from or why they believed as they did. In other words, I didn't take time to know them personally and listen to their story. I was more concerned about presenting a flawless dissertation that defended my faith rather than making a connection with them. My self-righteousness impeded me from living out the Great Commission of making disciples of all nations because my holy arrogance prevented me from encouraging other believers and connecting with non-believers.

WARNING: GOD FEELS DISTANT

From the outside, anyone would've thought I was the model Christian. I read my Bible faithfully, prayed regularly, lived an upright and moral lifestyle, was active in church, gave financially, and did my best at sharing my faith with others. However, in spite of my disciplined approach to the Christian faith, I began feeling more and more distant from God over time. I tried my best at practicing the Christian disciplines, but I knew I wasn't perfectly fulfilling them. I gave myself a lot of grace because I was trying to make a living and raise my family. Unfortunately, I wasn't paying attention to what was going on in my heart and soul, which is where the real problem was rooted. I desperately wanted the closeness and intimacy that I'd once had when I first committed my life to Christ, but something was off. I just couldn't figure out what it was.

When I felt distant from God, I would usually try to "do more" in order to feel closer to Him. By this time in my life, I'd been taught from different pastors at different churches from different denominations that reading the Bible more, praying more, and serving more was all I needed to do to experience a closer relationship with God. At times, "doing more" actually fostered intimacy with God. Yet at other times, I recognized that God could also feel distant when I was doing all of the right things with great effort and passion.

After recognizing that God felt distant irrespective of my doing the right things, I began to question the extent to which God is involved in this world. I started to view

God as somewhat aloof and detached. This false view of God led me to believe much of what we make of this world is up to the individual. I concluded that I might as well make the best of my life here on earth, which compelled me to pursue the American Dream even more. I rationalized that if God is distant from this world, what's the point in suffering here on earth. I might as well do the best I can at being a good citizen, helping others, and living comfortably. I believed that I could pursue all these things without overtly sinning against God.

Instead of dealing with the warning signs of God feeling distant, I began to believe that God was distant, even though it contradicts the truth found in the Bible. As such, I allowed my own circumstances to dictate what I believed about God instead of trusting the truth found in His word: "The Lord is near to the brokenhearted and saves those who are crushed in spirit" (Psalms 34:18). Had I dealt with the clear warning signs, I never would have fallen into the trap of thinking that intimacy with God was measured by doing all the right things. Instead of focusing on the Biblical truth of drawing near to God in order to experience a connection with Him, I focused more on doing the right things as a means of growing in my faith. I relied on my own ability and effort instead of abiding in Christ. My self-sufficiency led me down the path of a holy arrogance, and this caused me to be blinded by my own self-righteousness.

* * *

Because I was blinded by self-righteousness, I needed God to reveal it to me. Even more, I had to humble myself, agree with Him that I was, in fact, self-righteous, and ask Him to eliminate it from my life. As God awakened me to my self-righteousness, I discovered I couldn't take God's righteousness and "make it my own." Living righteously only comes from actively seeking and desiring God in humility and surrendering to His authority. As the Bible reveals, taking God's laws and attempting to follow them by our own effort and ability is to live by the law, and anyone who lives by the law will die by the law (Romans 2:12) no matter how pure, honest, and virtuous the person may be.

Now, instead of attempting to establish my own righteousness, I fully understand that, "Christ is the end of the law for righteousness for everyone who believes" (Romans 10:4). Words cannot describe how thankful I am that God used the pain of divorce to expose my self-righteousness. Because of His love for me, He gave me the opportunity to turn away from my distorted view of the Gospel. Otherwise, I would've continued as an American Pharisee—one who relies on their own righteousness to live out their faith. As we turn to God in humility, He will give us the strength we need, and as we begin to see our lives through the lens of humility, we will endure the trial and grow closer to God in the process.

* * *

Questions for Reflection:

1. Which cultural worldviews or sayings do you find particularly attractive? Why do you find them attractive?

2. If humility were measured to the degree in which we view ourselves in relation to God's essence and character, would God consider you humble?

3. In what areas of your life are you tempted to think more highly of yourself than you should?

4. Why is examining the attributes of God more effective at humbling us than trying to achieve humility by our own will and effort?

7

SURRENDER: EXPERIENCING FREEDOM

"There is a way which seems right to a man, but its end is the way of death." Proverbs 14:12

SUMMER 2010

*I*t was a hot July afternoon. The sun was shining as a few clouds speckled the deep blue sky, and a light breeze pushed our kayaks across the water. With my fishing line trolling in the water behind me, I looked over at Dad, who was about one hundred yards away, and as I motioned to the dock, I yelled to him, "I'm about ready to head in." Dad nodded and began paddling at an angle that closed the distance on both the dock and my kayak. I was paddling parallel to the shoreline when, suddenly, the nose of my kayak began to veer left towards the bank. I looked over my left shoulder and saw the tip of my pole bent all the way down into the water.

Assuming my crankbait was snagged on some debris, I pulled my rod out of its holder to let up on the tension, and all of a sudden, the pole almost jumped right out of my hand.

I knew it immediately—it was a muskie! I looked over at Dad and yelled, "I've got a big one!" I loosened the drag on my reel to make sure my line didn't snap, and this is when the fun really started. For the next twenty minutes, time stood still. I didn't think of anything but landing that fish. I was so focused on everything the fish was doing that I actually began to connect with it through my rod, reel, and line. I began to understand its behavior and could anticipate whether it was going to swim towards or away from me, dive down, or rise up. It was a time of intense concentration. Over and over again, I would reel in about ten yards of line, and then the giant fish would pull the line right back out making the spool on my reel buzz like an electric drill.

The fish was so strong that it was literally pulling my kayak through the water. At one point, the fish was so angry that it jumped out of the water and landed on my dad's kayak—he had to beat it off with his paddle! The fish was flopping around in a fury, and my dad, out of desperation to keep away from its razor-sharp teeth, shoved the fish off the nose of his kayak with the paddle. I was shocked that Dad was even able to stay upright in his kayak! Finally, as the fish began to tire out, I managed to paddle myself to shore and land the fish. It was my largest fresh water catch—a 36-inch muskie caught on a weak twelve-pound fishing line with no leader. It was a fisherman's miracle because the crankbait was hooked perfectly into the side of the mouth, which made the fish unable to bite the line. I could only admire the fish for a few brief seconds because it was so worn out. I quickly put it back in the water and watched it swim way. I often wonder if that fish has ever been caught again, and if so, did it put up an even bigger fight than the one I experienced.

Muskie are known as "the fish of 10,000 casts," and very few people ever have the opportunity to catch one. Those who do get the rare opportunity will never forget the experience.

These fish have a pre-historic look to them and possess many layers of teeth that will shred anything they bite. As such, extreme care needs to be taken when handling them. Simply put, these fish are fresh water monsters.

This experience goes down as the greatest fishing story I will ever be able to tell. As much as I fish, I may very well catch a larger fish, but even bigger fish will never compare to my encounter with that muskie. I have a special attachment to this particular fish because, just a moment before I hooked it, I was lost in the quiet suspension as I floated atop the water and wondered if God even existed. From my pit of helplessness and hopelessness, God appeared, God answered, and God showed He existed by allowing me to experience the greatest fishing story of my life. In that empty silence of brokenness, the wind was actually drifting me back to Him. In fact, He was there with me all the time.

But catching this fish wasn't even the real beauty of this story. It's not about the size of the fish, the type of fish, or even the miracle of catching such a difficult fish at the very moment I was questioning God's existence. The greatest beauty was in those twenty minutes it took me to catch that fish. For those twenty minutes, I forgot about all of the sorrow, all of the hurt, and all of the despair of my broken marriage. It was literally the first time in three weeks that I'd been able to shift my focus completely off of my terrible circumstances. And as I released that fish back into the water, I knew without a doubt that God, in His lovingkindness, provided that unforgettable moment. So, even though my circumstances did not change, my perspective changed dramatically. In that moment, I realized I didn't worship a God who will always prevent pain and suffering from occurring at my beck and call. I worship a God who chooses to walk through the pain with me and who will never leave me or forsake me. And

I didn't believe this truth just because I had read it in the Bible—I believed it because I'd now experienced it firsthand.

From that moment, I knew God would be with me regardless of whether or not Alyson went through with the divorce. At the lowest point of my life, part of me died, and yet I was simultaneously being renewed by my Creator. In His perfect love for me, God broke me down by allowing the consequences of divorce to reveal a much bigger and more pervasive problem—I was an American Pharisee. He allowed pain and suffering into my life to grab my attention and bring me to the point of complete dependency on Him.

WHAT IS TRUE FREEDOM?

The pursuit of success leads to a constant fear of failure. The pursuit of sex leads to a constant fear of being unfulfilled. The pursuit of comfort leads to a constant fear of pain. The pursuit of beauty leads to a constant fear of rejection. Even when trying to find freedom in noble causes such as serving those who are less fortunate, protecting the environment, and focusing on the family, these can all be rooted in the fear of being insignificant. Virtually anything a person pursues to find freedom—other than Christ—will eventually lead to some form of bondage. Left unchecked, these pursuits will lead to broken relationships, isolation, and loneliness.

Why is this the case? It's because people are seeking freedom from something that ultimately entraps them. It is one of the strangest ironies known to mankind. The more desperate, motivated, and intense our pursuit of personal freedom becomes, the more elusive contentment becomes. As Solomon stated, "I have seen all the works which have been done under the sun, and behold, all is vanity and striving after wind" (Ecclesiastes 1:14). In this short statement, Solomon provides a clear illustration of the futility and hopelessness of elevating ourselves by pursuing our natural desires. We are simply left empty and unfulfilled. Yet time and time again, we find ourselves "following our heart" down the path that leads to this very emptiness. Our culture even encourages us to take the journey that ultimately leads to unfulfillment and desolation. Here are just a few of the common expressions we hear:

> VIRTUALLY ANYTHING A PERSON PURSUES TO FIND FREEDOM—OTHER THAN CHRIST—WILL EVENTUALLY LEAD TO SOME FORM OF BONDAGE.

- Never let anyone get in the way of your dreams

- You are free to be anything you want to be

- Follow your heart and give it your all

- Be your own boss

- Life is what you make it

Here's the underlying premise behind all of these sayings: "You are in charge of your own destiny. If you want to find freedom, it is up to you to define what freedom looks like. Then go after it." In essence, we are the rulers of our own kingdom, so we get to call the shots. After all, freedom is being able to do whatever we want, whenever we want, and however we want. This is an enticing path, but it's one that ultimately leads you to become a slave of what you pursue.

America was founded upon independence, and this tradition of independence has been carried down from generation to generation. Over two hundred years later,

Americans have taken independence to an unhealthy extreme. If we are subject to anyone, we perceive it as oppression and a barrier to our personal liberty, and we are bombarded with this message through marketing, media, and motivational speakers. "Do whatever makes you happy" has become our cultural mantra. From the world's standpoint, happiness is the end goal of humanity, so this belief perfectly aligns with anyone who believes this world is the only thing we have. Even more, this thinking tells us that the greatest satisfaction we could ever receive is to enjoy the "here and now," and we live for what is immediately in front of us. Happiness has become the end goal, and man's definition of freedom—to be the ruler of our lives—is the means by which we obtain this happiness. All we have to do is follow our hearts because the answer lies within us.

But what does the Bible tell us? The prophet Jeremiah states, "The heart is more deceitful than all else and is desperately sick; Who can understand it?" (Jeremiah 17:9). As God's Word reveals, if we seek the answer that lies within us, then we will certainly be led astray because our hearts deceive us. In other words, our hearts deceive us into thinking that happiness is the end goal of life and that all we have to live for is the here and now. Even those who claim a saving faith in Jesus are constantly being tempted to follow their hearts instead of following Jesus. We fall into the trap of following the world's view that power provides control, control provides independence, independence provides freedom, and freedom provides happiness. So, we fight for our rights and try to win at any cost with the hope of experiencing the good life on earth, but in doing so, we lose sight of the eternal perspective.

THE BATTLE FOR CONTROL

Our desire for control prevents us from surrendering to Christ's authority as Lord. Humans are by nature strong-willed. We want our way, and we want it immediately. We think we know what's best, so we sit on our throne of judgment declaring what is good and what is evil. Sadly, our judgment is skewed towards our own interests and pursuits. We declare anything that helps us establish our kingdom is "good," and anything that prevents us from establishing out kingdom is "evil." We spend countless hours trying to control our destiny and completely miss the fact that God is the One who is ultimately in control. Even if we intellectually know that God is in control, we often behave otherwise and will take great measures to ensure *our* kingdom comes and *our* will is done. Since no one else knows what we need and when we need it better than our own hearts, control provides us a sense of comfort. And while we may not admit it with our words, our actions demonstrate that we think we know what's in our best interests better than God. We are deceived into thinking that pursuing something other than God will bring us satisfaction. The reality is that we will be left disappointed and unfulfilled.

This desire to control our own destiny goes all the way back to the Garden of Eden. God gave Adam one simple command...just one. He said, "From any tree of the garden you may eat freely; but from the tree of the knowledge of good and evil you shall not eat, for in the day that you eat from it you will surely die" (Genesis 2:16-17). In the Garden, Adam and Eve lived in a world full of "yeses" and only one "no"—don't eat from a certain tree.

Just a little later, we begin to see how well they did following God's one and only command:

"Now the serpent was more crafty than any beast of the field which the Lord God had made. And he said to the woman, 'Indeed, has God said, 'You shall not eat from any tree in the garden'?' The woman said to the serpent, 'From the fruit of the trees of the garden we may eat; but from the fruit of the tree which is in the middle of the garden, God has said, 'You shall not eat from it or touch it, or you will die." The serpent said to the woman, 'You surely will not die! For God knows that in the day you eat from it your eyes will be opened, and you will be like God, knowing good and evil.' When the woman saw that the tree was good for food, and that it was a delight to the eyes, and that the tree was desirable to make one wise, she took from its fruit and ate; and she gave also to her husband with her, and he ate. Then the eyes of both of them were opened, and they knew that they were naked; and they sewed fig leaves together and made themselves loin coverings." (Genesis 3:1-7)

Sadly, Adam and Eve couldn't handle God's one "no," and the world has been living with the consequences ever since. All of the world's brokenness originated with Adam, and yet Adam's struggle is our struggle. This struggle can be summed up in these simple truths:

1. Like Adam, we believe God is withholding something good from us. Otherwise, we would never give into temptation.

2. Like Adam, we believe we know better than God. Otherwise, we would never disobey.

3. Like Adam, we want to be like God. Otherwise, we would live completely surrendered to His rule without any struggle.

For Eve, at the core of her disobedience was also the belief that God was withholding something good from her. She believed she knew better than God by thinking wisdom was worth the price of death. Instead of being content to bear the image of God, she wanted to be like God, knowing good and evil. And while Eve was the first to disobey, Adam was ultimately at fault because he was standing right beside Eve and did nothing to stop her. He was completely passive and watched the entire interaction between the serpent and Eve take place. His passivity not only showed a lack of love for Eve, but it also led to his own demise. Instead of being strong and standing up for what God said, his passivity revealed his halfhearted attitude towards God's instruction.

And not much has changed ever since the fall of Adam. People still possess this inherent belief that God is some kind of killjoy. They think God's commands are nothing but a list of dos and don'ts that have no relevance to their own lives. They disregard the responsibilities that God has given them. They want, more than anything, to be their own god. And it should come as no surprise that people who don't follow Christ would naturally gravitate towards this kind of living. However, it is shocking that many who claim a faith in Jesus are still living the same as those who don't claim faith. It's as if they have confessed Jesus as their savior, but they have not been changed by God's grace.

If we desire to be in control of our lives rather than allowing God to direct our paths, then we are fighting and rebelling against God. If we want what we want, instead of what God wants for us, then we are resisting God's best regardless of what we say we believe. If we approach our relationship to Christ with the attitude of, "What can He do for me?" then we are more interested in personal gain than a personal relationship with Him. If we profess with our mouths that we are committed to following Christ, yet stop serving the moment it becomes inconvenient or doesn't align with how we want to serve, then we are more committed to our agenda than to God's agenda. If we say we have "accepted Christ into our hearts" and yet continue to live independently from Him, then we cannot say we are following Christ.

If we truly believe God is omniscient and the source of everything good, then common sense tells us we should follow Him and do what He says. By surrendering our plan for God's plan, we discover that true freedom is found within the eternal realm of God's kingdom. It is God who designed freedom, and in His lovingkindness, He wants us to experience this freedom. With this understanding, we begin to see God's commands as a reflection of His character, instead of seeing them as a list of rules. We begin to see His laws as parameters for living in the freedom that He designed for us, instead of restrictions that prevent us from doing what we prefer. It almost seems like a contradiction that surrendering our lives to God will produce freedom. But Jesus makes this point very clear in Luke 9:24 where He states, "For whoever wishes to save his life will lose it, but whoever loses his life for My sake, he is the one who will save it."

THE ROOT OF CONTROL IS PRIDE

Since humility is required for surrender, and pride opposes humility, then pride becomes the greatest barrier to surrender. Pride prevents us from experiencing a close and intimate relationship with God. It's not that man's pride is greater or more powerful than God, but rather we are intentionally rejecting God because of our pride. By definition, pride says we prefer our ways, our thoughts, our desires, and ourselves to others. As such, pride is a relationship killer. To prefer oneself to God is to reject the reality of God's majesty. This is precisely why American Pharisees go through much of their lives experiencing a God who is distant, aloof, and uninvolved in their lives—He becomes a rigid God who is far away instead of an intimate God who is near. American Pharisees are unable to obtain a right view of God because they are preoccupied with themselves.

If we allow pride to get in the way of our relationship with God, the Bible says He will oppose us and withhold His grace from us (I Peter 5:5). Could it be that many people who claim a faith in Jesus have not actually experienced the freedom offered by Christ simply because their pride is getting in the way? Once we begin to appreciate the freedom found in God's grace, we cannot help but humbly respond by giving up control of our lives and surrendering to His sovereignty. And here is the key difference between man's attempt at surrendering his will before God and true authentic surrender to God—the former is rooted in pride (the belief that one is capable of complete surrender) and the other is rooted in humility (seeing God for who He really is and responding to Him accordingly).

Since our hearts are filled with desires that ultimately lead to emptiness and unfulfillment, we need to allow God to fill our hearts with Himself. We cannot make this happen through our own will, which is why we must allow His love to penetrate our hearts. Once His love changes our hearts, we cannot help but respond in surrender to His will. If we use our own willpower to surrender, then, at any given point in time, we can choose again *not* to surrender. In doing so, our pride creeps in, and we remain in control of ourselves instead of giving control to God.

So, what's the answer to defeating the pride that pollutes our lives? It's not a matter of trying harder to surrender our will to Christ's authority—that will never work long-term. The key to defeating pride is to center our hearts and minds on God alone: to sit in wonder of His infinite majesty, to ponder the power of His sovereignty, to dwell upon His lovingkindness. Since our nature is to turn away from God instead of turning towards Him, we must humbly ask God to reveal Himself to us so that we can gain a better picture of who He is. Only then will we begin to see how big God is and how small we really are. This is where true authentic surrender begins.

GOD IS THE END GOAL OF THE GOSPEL

The sole purpose of the Gospel is for God to be glorified; however, American Pharisees have fallen into the misguided theology that mankind is the end goal of the Gospel. This line of thinking elevates man above God as we view our faith from a self-centered perspective. The truth is that God is the end goal of the Gospel. He demonstrated His love for us by providing a way back to Him through Jesus. He is the One to be glorified above all else because of His goodness toward mankind. In his book *Radical,* David Platt writes about this very idea:

> We live in a church culture that has a dangerous tendency to disconnect the grace of God from the glory of God. Our hearts resonate with the idea of enjoying God's grace. We bask in sermons, conferences, and books that exalt a grace centering on us. And while the wonder of grace is worthy of our attention, if that grace is disconnected from its purpose, the sad result

is a self-centered Christianity that bypasses the heart of God.[4]

While it is true that we are saved by God's grace, the end goal of God's grace is for Him to be glorified—not ourselves. If we prefer sitting along the sidelines as we enjoy God's grace rather than getting in the game of glorifying Him, then we have used His grace for a purpose for which it was never designed. Reading the Bible to find an answer that matches my agenda and praying for my wishes to come true is a needs-seeking religion that says the Gospel is all about my security, my comfort, my success, my well-being, and my enjoyment. Our American culture of consumerism has quietly crept into our faith and made faith all about us, but God has a different perspective:

> "It is not for your sake, O house of Israel, that I am going to do these things, **but for the sake of My holy name**" (Ezekiel 36:22).

> "I, even I, am the one who wipes out your transgressions for **My own sake**" (Isaiah 43:25).

God's Word is clear that His plan of salvation has been accomplished because He is glorious; He is magnificent; He is to be exalted.

How we respond to God says a lot about our love for Him. Where do God's plans intersect with our plans? Are they an after-thought, carefully considered, or directing our focus? Do we view His promptings as optional or mandatory? If we're feeling "led by the Spirit," are we truly committed, viewing this leading as a "must obey" with no wavering, or are we only conditionally committed? Proverbs 19:21 states, "Many plans are in a man's heart, but the counsel of the Lord will stand." Are you focused on your plans or God's counsel? Your plans could be very noble; however, if your plans are apart from God's counsel or if you're only considering God's counsel to see how it benefits you, then you're following your own agenda and not God's.

In the height of my American Pharisee days, I believed I was following God's will for my life—but I was really following my own agenda. I took the ever popular, "What Would Jesus Do?" question and applied it in a way that didn't violate God's law and promoted my agenda of the good and nice life. For example, I used this rationale when I was pursuing law school. I was drawn to law because I wanted to have a positive influence in the legal system. I prayed a lot about the decision because it was a significant commitment, and I remember asking God if this was the direction I should go. But I never really received any real confirmation. So, I convinced myself that becoming an attorney was my civic duty, as I would provide justice in an otherwise corrupt world. I rationalized my decision by telling myself, "Why wouldn't God want me to be an attorney? I'm committed to doing what's right. I would fight for the innocent and those who were wronged."

> THE KEY TO DEFEATING PRIDE IS TO CENTER OUR HEARTS AND MINDS ON GOD ALONE: TO SIT IN WONDER OF HIS INFINITE MAJESTY, TO PONDER THE POWER OF HIS SOVEREIGNTY, TO DWELL UPON HIS LOVINGKINDNESS.

Instead of seeking self-serving answers to questions about God's will, I should have humbled myself, surrendered my plan, and sought guidance from God, but instead I played the role of God by promoting my own agenda. Even if He continued to be silent, I should have been better aligned to His agenda and sensed that law school was not a wise decision. I was already experiencing long hours and stress at work, and I wasn't paying attention to Alyson and Meredith's needs. Even more, when I was at home, I was disconnected from them because of the numerous responsibilities I'd committed to outside the home. I was at home physically, but I was absent relationally and emotionally.

Had my priorities been truly focused on God first and family second, I would have quickly known that my pursuit of law school was promoting my agenda and wasn't in the best interest of my connection with God or my family. My failure to recognize this caused even more distance between Alyson and me. In hindsight, I'm so thankful God forced me to drop out of law school because of my back injury. It was that specific event that caused me to rethink my priorities, and I began taking intentional steps of surrendering my pursuit of success and achievement. Unfortunately, these changes were too late to save my marriage. Besides, I still hadn't fully surrendered to God. I'd just decided to begin pursuing my family over my career and was still practicing my faith on my own and disconnected from God.

We cannot begin to experience the freedom God has established for us until we surrender ourselves to His authority and allow Him to direct our paths (Proverbs 16:9). Once we have surrendered to Him, we can then begin to walk down the path He originally intended for us. God used suffering to teach me that the Christian life was never meant to be something that I had to figure out or even conquer on my own. He showed me that the Christian life was always meant to be one in which we allow God to work in us and through us. My painful divorce drew me closer to Him and helped me realize that life is not about me being glorified—it's about God being glorified, no matter the circumstance.

* * *

Questions for Reflection:

1. What area(s) of your life are you struggling to surrender to God?

2. How is this resistance to surrender negatively impacting your connection with God? With those who are closest to you?

3. How will focusing on God's majesty bring you closer to authentic surrender?

8

OBEDIENCE:
THE EXPRESSION OF LOVE

"If you love me, you will keep my commandments."
John 14:15

JULY 2014

While fishing under the shade tree at Alum Creek, I continued to reflect on how I became an American Pharisee. I realized this transition didn't happen overnight but rather was a slow fade that occurred over a long period of time. As I experienced success throughout my life, I gradually began to connect the fruits of my success to my faith. I learned at a young age that a job well done would be rewarded, so I began to combine this worldview with my faith. I started to believe the material blessings that God provided were dependent upon my performing the Christian disciplines such as studying my Bible, praying, living morally upright, attending church, serving faithfully, giving generously, and sharing the Gospel. If I continued to grow and improve spiritually, I believed I would find favor with God, and He would reward me with material blessings. I was aware that my salvation was by faith alone, and I could do nothing to earn the gift of eternal life. But somewhere along the way, I began holding onto the misguided belief that connected my spiritual performance to God's material blessing. If I was obedient in pursuing the Christian disciplines in increasing measure, I believed God would continue to bless me with what I wanted here on earth. But as I continued to pursue the American Dream, my relationship with Jesus became distant. The more disciplined I became at practicing my faith, the more distant He felt from my life.

In my striving to be the perfect husband, father, friend, worker, and citizen, I didn't leave any time or energy to be what God had actually called me to be—His child. The more I focused on every other role in my life, the less I focused on my true identity in Christ. I created a distorted picture of the "American Christian." In my mind, an American Christian had a good education, a good career, a good family, a nice car, a nice house, and a nice retirement plan. It was a person who was saved by grace but also worked hard at sinning less and serving God with the hope that life on earth would turn out okay. The problem with this distorted view is that it's simply not consistent with Scripture.

Jesus tells us that in order to follow Him we are to die to ourselves each and every day. We are to lose our lives, so we can find them. New Testament believers who followed Jesus were persecuted, tortured, and imprisoned because of their faith. They did not live comfortably, nor did they pursue a comfortable lifestyle. They truly knew what it meant to delight themselves in the Lord, which is why they were willing to endure hardship. Instead of practicing their faith, they lived out their faith by resting in their identity as children of God. Knowing who they were in Christ was all they needed to sustain them through any hardship or suffering. They understood that suffering precedes glory, and they were *willing to be obedient regardless of the circumstances—not for the sake of obedience, but for the sake of Christ's glory.*

After the divorce, I took a completely different approach to obedience. I no longer pursued obedience as the means to material reward. I no longer focused on obedience for obedience's sake. Instead, I focused on my identity in Christ, and my obedience became a natural response of my love for Him. I began to view morality and behavior modification as man's futile attempt to "do right," and many believers, including myself, have fallen into this trap. I now recognize and rest in the truth that God has already made me right through His Son. All I have to do is abide in Christ and obedience will be the natural outflow of His righteousness at work within me. Instead of always focusing on doing the right thing, I now focus on doing the wise thing—allowing Christ to change my heart by dying to self and living for Christ.

* * *

As I sat under that shade tree enjoying the solitude and appreciating the gift of the outdoors, I was overwhelmed by a deep sense of gratitude. I was so grateful to be alive and to experience this simple moment in time. I was also grateful for what the Lord had taught me about obedience over these last few years. Even though I didn't catch any fish, this was one of the most memorable moments of my life because it was my first time fishing after I'd almost died.

Just a few weeks earlier, I was scheduled to go on a mission trip to Jamaica with a group of people from Lifepoint Church. The decision to go was not spontaneous by any means. I had spent several months praying and seeking wisdom from trusted friends to determine whether or not this was God's timing for me to go. I eventually decided to go and was confident

I'd made the right decision. I believed that going on this specific trip was simply a matter of obedience.

On the day before I was scheduled to leave for Jamaica, I went into work, but I wasn't feeling well. While walking from the parking lot into the office, I started to breathe heavily, my heart began beating rapidly, and I broke out into a cold sweat. I knew these symptoms should have caused concern, but I proceeded to my office anyway. Later that morning, I met with a colleague of mine. His face looked concerned, and he said, "Kevin, you don't look so good. Are you feeling okay?" After I said that I wasn't doing too well, he advised me to leave immediately and go to the doctor to get checked out.

Upon his advice, I took an early lunch and decided to drive myself to an Urgent Care facility. As I was driving, I remember thinking that I should just go home and rest. But as I approached the Urgent Care facility, I decided to go in anyway, just to rule out anything serious. Since I was leaving for Jamaica the next morning, I wanted to make sure I was in good health.

Much to my surprise, everything was not okay. The physician immediately ordered me to the nearest ER for further testing. Within an hour at the ER, the doctors determined that I had a bilateral pulmonary embolism, and I was admitted into the hospital for an emergency procedure to break the blood clot that was lodged in both of my lungs. I remember telling the cardiologist that I was leaving for Jamaica the next morning and asked him if I would be cleared to go. He replied, "If you go on that trip, you will not make it back alive."

Through my entire stay at the hospital and even after I finally came home, I never really comprehended the gravity of my situation. It wasn't until I was sitting under that shade tree that I truly understood the reality of what had occurred—I would have died if it weren't for my trip to Jamaica. That mission trip was the sole reason I even decided to check myself into the Urgent Care. Had I not been going to Jamaica, I would have gone home to rest and never woken up.

I always knew obedience to God was important, but now I learned that responding to His calling could literally be a matter of life or death.

* * *

OBEY GOD

Take a moment to consider your first thoughts and emotions when you hear the words "obey God." How we react to this statement reveals much about our view of God. Many people think that obeying God means they have an obligation to comply with God's rules, and, as such, they need to work hard to follow them. So, they put their primary focus on behavior modification and sin management in the hopes of living a morally upright life. After repeated attempts of trying hard, doing well for a while, and ultimately failing somewhere along the way, they get discouraged and begin seeing obedience as a burden. Experiencing the weight of this burden, they begin to view God's Law in a negative light and see God as an unpleasant Taskmaster with unrealistic demands.

Obeying God shouldn't be such a burden. Yet, if we possess a negative view of obedience, then we can be assured that our view of God's Law will be distorted. Obedience should be viewed as a natural reflex that results from our love of God and desire to be in a close relationship with Him. As we abide in Christ, our lives are transformed, and we will find ourselves living in His righteousness—not our own. Temptation begins to fade away because our desire for God becomes stronger than the desire for self-fulfillment. Our view of God changes from an unpleasant Taskmaster to a compassionate Caregiver who helps us experience the true freedom contained within the boundaries of His Law. This freedom is experienced through obedience.

MOTIVATED BY DUTY AND OBLIGATION

Many believers are motivated to obey out of a sense of duty or obligation. Something within them says they must "do better" at conducting their lives in a manner consistent with God's Law. This can lead a well-meaning believer into thinking compliance to God's laws is the primary method of successfully obeying God. This is best represented by a person's eliminating bad habits and replacing them with good habits—ones that are consistent with the Bible. The person will try their best at implementing the Christian disciplines such as reading the Bible, praying, attending church, serving, and tithing. As time goes on, the person attempts to perform all of these disciplines in increasing measure and hopes to grow in their faith. Much of this "do more" is rooted in self-motivation, self-discipline, and self-discovery instead of allowing the Holy Spirit to transform the heart. The end result is a person who is relying on self to practice their faith instead of relying on the Holy Spirit to live out the faith that God is actively working within the individual.

Much of this misguided approach to obedience is rooted in our American culture. Society convinces us we should strive to be "the best version of ourselves," and so we work tirelessly in every area of life—including our faith. On the surface, working hard to be a better person appears to be a noble goal. After all, the world needs more love, joy, peace, patience, kindness, goodness, faithfulness, gentleness, and self-control. We believe that if we work hard, then we can achieve any goal we desire; thus, we attempt to live a virtuous life in the hopes of producing the fruit of the Spirit. Our independent, self-sufficient, and results-driven American mindset fools us into thinking that we can actually produce the fruit of the Spirit. So, we work tirelessly to produce fruit—only we can't. The Bible is clear that it's impossible through human means to produce the fruit of the Spirit that Paul describes in Galatians 5:22-23.

Remember, the Bible says no one is righteous. If that's true, then we cannot produce the fruit of the Spirit. Sure, we might convince ourselves into thinking that we are peaceful, patient, and kind human beings. We may feel very good about ourselves for a period of time and even rationalize that we are having a positive influence in the world. But in reality, we are only suppressing our own hostility, intolerance, and cruelty as we attempt to be the best version of ourselves. This is why non-believers can appear morally upright and why believers can be deceived into thinking they are virtuous. They are relying on their own efforts to suppress their own wickedness instead of bearing the fruit of the Spirit. No matter how hard we try, we can never become the person God originally created us to be through our own effort. Godliness only comes from God; we cannot produce it.

> OUR INDEPENDENT, SELF-SUFFICIENT, AND RESULTS-DRIVEN AMERICAN MINDSET FOOLS US INTO THINKING THAT WE CAN ACTUALLY PRODUCE THE FRUIT OF THE SPIRIT.

HOW PHARISEES VIEW THE LAW

Still, American Pharisees actually believe they can attain godliness by obeying God's commands. They chase after noble and virtuous pursuits to the point that their so-called morality creates a wedge in their relationship with God because they are pursuing righteousness more than God. They worship morality and virtue over worshiping God. For example, they'll read the Bible like an instruction manual to life and attempt to live out what they've read. With this thinking comes a lack of awareness about their sinful heart. While a person of good moral character may commit fewer sins than the corrupt person, at the core of their being, *both* possess the same broken, flawed heart. And our flawed hearts want to be both judge and jury of our own lives. In doing so, people wrongfully take God's rightful place as Judge.

The Pharisees of Jesus' day possessed this same mentality. They believed they were righteous based on their compliance to the laws. They became their own judges to gauge how well they were obeying God. By reconciling their actions against their interpretation of God's laws, they created their own barometer of morality, and in their self-righteousness, they rejected Jesus because they preferred their "righteous living" over a relationship with Christ.

Pursuing righteous living can be a tricky topic to understand because, as Paul writes in Philippians, we must work out our salvation with fear and trembling (Philippians 2:12). When I was living the American Pharisee life, I thought this meant that once we accept Christ as our Lord, it was up to us to do the best we can at living the Christian life. I knew that I wasn't working for my salvation, because I was saved by God's grace, but I did think that working out my salvation was up to me. So, I tried to be the best person I could and focused a considerable amount of effort on self-improvement and self-help. I didn't see anything wrong with this approach because our American culture promotes this very ideal and rewards those who are virtuous, disciplined, motivated, and focused. As I continued to 'work out my salvation', I began relying more on my own efforts and depending less upon God. I never confessed this to anyone because I didn't see any harm in making myself a better person. Eventually, my "doing good" got in the way of thinking I needed God. I became more independent in my decisions, relied on my own discernment to figure out 'what would Jesus do', and based this on my own understanding of the Bible. While I may have been living a more virtuous life than a criminal, I was, in reality, no different because I was relying on my own judgment to determine what I should and should not do. I may have been walking in obedience to the law, but I was not walking in obedience to faith as Paul describes in Romans 1:5 and 16:26. Instead of living in the reality that I was saved by grace and sanctified by grace, I believed I was saved by grace and sanctified by works.

Much of my misguided thinking came from the fact that I completely missed what Paul said *after* Philippians 2:12. In the very next verse (v13), Paul states, "For it is God who is at work in you both to will and to work for His good pleasure." I missed *God's* role in my faith. The only explanation I have for completely missing this verse is that I was too focused on interpreting Scripture on my own terms, instead of allowing God to reveal Himself to me through His Word. Now that I see how verse 13 ties into verse 12, it all makes sense. My identity is in Christ; therefore, I died to myself, and I am made alive in Him. Because my identity is now in Christ, God is actively working in me. The salvation that I'm working out is the salvation that God is actively working within me. My understanding this great truth creates a sense of awe and trembling within me.

MERE COMPLIANCE TO THE RULES

Before I began desiring God with a true passion, I had a tendency to view God's law as burdensome. I was able to follow the "don'ts" without too much difficulty, but it was the "dos" that became a burden to me. Reading the Bible, praying, attending church, serving, tithing, and sharing the Gospel were disciplines that I knew all healthy Christians do on a consistent basis, so I did them and did them well from a performance standpoint.

Eventually, these disciplines became burdensome. Sure, I experienced moments of real spiritual growth. But for the most part, I felt burdened by them. I never really talked to anyone about my pessimistic views and feelings of apathy towards my faith. I knew those views and feelings were wrong, so I thought this was all part of my personal spiritual journey to figure out on my own. I didn't realize it at the time, but my spiritual independence was really just pride being influenced by my pursuit of the American Dream. I relied on my own efforts to grow spiritually instead of relying on God to transform me. As I traveled down this path, God became distant and for good reason. I was trying to live out my faith on my own effort and only allowing God in the picture when I needed Him. I was pursuing a needs-seeking relationship with my Creator.

Unfortunately, it's easy to fall into the trap of simply obeying the commandments because "God said so." This attitude leads to a compliance approach to God's laws. Obedience out of mere compliance is an indication that we are giving God the bare minimum of ourselves. We carry the attitude that says, "Just tell me what You want me to do, and I'll do it," which is quite possibly one of the weakest expressions of love. In essence, we are saying, "Tell me what to do, and I'll do it, so I can then continue pursuing my own desires." True love desires and pursues, but compliance merely says, "I'm only willing to do the bare minimum in order for this relationship to work."

Instead of focusing on righteous living, I should have been focusing on my identity in Christ. Had I recognized that I am justified and sanctified by Christ alone, in doing so,

> I RELIED ON MY OWN EFFORTS TO GROW SPIRITUALLY INSTEAD OF RELYING ON GOD TO TRANSFORM ME.

my love for God would have been expressed through obedience. But the more I viewed the commandments as mere rules, the more I used my own knowledge, ability, and effort to live by those rules.

OBEY TO RECEIVE

Not only did I try to obey the commandments by my own effort through compliance, I also obeyed with the motive of hoping to receive something from God. I now see this mindset leads to a sense of entitlement. Throughout my American Pharisee life, I dedicated a significant amount of time and energy to growing spiritually and serving in numerous capacities because I naturally assumed that God would bless me with the "good and nice" life in return for my hard work. Thus, I obeyed the commandments for obedience's sake and not for Christ's sake. Much of this misguided mindset comes from our worldview that we "do good and are rewarded." If we do good and things don't work out the way we planned, then we falsely conclude that God has somehow failed us.

The Apostle James aptly summarizes what this looks like at a general level:

> You ask and do not receive, because **you ask with wrong motives**, so that you may spend it on your pleasures. **You adulteresses**, do you not know that friendship with the world is hostility toward God? Therefore, whoever wishes to be a friend of the world makes himself an enemy of God. Or do you think that the Scripture speaks to no purpose: 'He jealously desires the Spirit which He has made to dwell in us'? But He gives a greater grace. Therefore, it says, '**God is opposed to the proud, but gives grace to the humble**.' Submit therefore to God. **Resist the devil and he will flee from you. Draw near to God, and He will draw near to you**. (James 4:3-8)

James' words speak clearly—we ask with wrong motives when we seek God to promote our own agenda, our own self-sufficiency, and our desires regardless of how virtuous they might appear. When we promote self over God, we are betraying our original commitment to God, which is why James uses the term "adulteresses." Interestingly, God often uses the term "adulteresses" to describe the betrayal of our commitment to Him. If we obey God's commands simply because we experience the benefits of doing the right thing, then our primary motive for obedience is self-serving and we're not obeying God out of love. We are seeking a performance-based blessing, and in doing so, we commit adultery against Him.

Even though I did "all the right things," my motives were usually for selfish gain. Similar to the Pharisees, I did all the right things for all the wrong reasons. My motives weren't 100% selfish 100% of the time, but it takes less than 0.000001% selfishness to distort our view of the Gospel. I now realize that God owes me nothing—He has already given me everything that has eternal worth. Sadly, I even used Scripture to justify my actions as I convinced myself that God would bless my efforts if I honored Him. Some of my favorite verses were:

"Delight yourself in the Lord, and He will give you the desires of your heart" (Psalms 37:4).

"He who trusts in the Lord will prosper" (Proverbs 28:25).

"For I know the plans I have for you,' declares the Lord, 'plans for welfare and not for calamity to give you a future and a hope" (Jeremiah 29:11).

"The Lord will give strength to His people; The Lord will bless His people with peace" (Psalms 29:11).

Every one of these verses is true, but I viewed them through the lens of the earthly and material instead of the heavenly and eternal. My heart desired the American Dream, and I was convinced that God would give me the strength to experience a peaceful life full of joy here and now. I became confident that God would be faithful and bless my hard work as long as I was dedicated to serving Him and giving Him the credit for my personal success. And, just like some of the believers from my childhood church, I also found myself following the non-biblical traditions of the American Pharisee.

LOVE: THE RIGHT MOTIVATION

Obedience is a matter of loving God. If asked, I imagine most everyone who claims a faith in Jesus Christ will naturally say, "I love God." But how do you express your love to God? Jesus said, "If you love me, you will keep my commandments" (John 14:15). A few verses later, He emphasizes this point again: "If anyone loves me, he will keep My word; and My Father will love him, and We will come to him and make Our abode with him." For some reason, many people lose sight of the truth that obedience is the expression of love. It is not the source of love. Likewise, good works are not the means to salvation as shown in Romans 3:20 and 4:5, but rather the fulfillment of salvation (Eph. 2:10).

If I view the commandments as rules, I will see God as a Taskmaster. But if I view God's commandments as a description of His very nature, then I will desire to live in obedience to the Law as I recognize my identity in Christ and pursue Him. One reason His law has been given is it enables us to gain a better understanding of His character—who He is and how He operates. Understanding that God's law is a reflection of Him, we recognize there is no way we can fulfill His law unless His very nature is living within us. As our love for God and for others comes to maturity, we begin fulfilling the Law and Commandments. Jesus spoke of this very thing in the book of Matthew:

> And He [Jesus] said to him, 'You shall love the Lord your God with all of your heart, with all of your soul, and with all of your mind. This is the great and foremost commandment. The second is like it, 'You shall love your neighbor as yourself.' **On these two**

commandments depend the whole Law and the Prophets. (Matthew 22:37-40)

As the Scriptures reveal, the more I love God, the more I desire to live according to His commands. John Piper makes a similar observation about obeying God's commandments:

> The challenge before us is not merely to do what God says because He is God, but to desire what God says because He is good. The challenge is not merely to pursue righteousness, but to prefer righteousness. The challenge is to get up in the morning and prayerfully meditate on the Scriptures until we experience joy and peace in believing the "precious and very great promises" of God (2 Peter 1:4). With this joy set before us, the commandments of God will not be burdensome. (1 John 5:3), and the compensation of sin will appear too brief and too shallow to lure us.[5]

We learn more about God's Law in the book of Romans when Paul states that the Law is holy, righteous, and good (Romans 7:11-13). It is our opposition to the Law or attempting to live by the Law that condemns every human being.

To help ensure my motives are based on loving God instead of loving righteousness, I now ask myself the following questions on regular basis:

- Do I desire the commandments because He is good?

- Am I being transformed by what the Bible is telling me?

- Is prayer changing my heart?

- Am I beginning to see the world through God's eyes and meeting Him where He actively works in the lives of others?

If the answer to any of these questions is a "no" or "I'm not sure," I no longer try harder to fix my attitude. Instead, I focus on loving God with all my heart, soul, and mind. As my love for God increases, my love for sin decreases.

DESIRING GOD

The life we pursue is based on what we truly desire. So, the question we should constantly be asking ourselves is this, "Am I desiring anything over God?" If so, we can be assured we are committing adultery against Him. We must remember that true freedom comes from God alone, and this freedom is discovered when we commit our lives to God in repentance and faith. As we express our commitment to God through humility, surrender, and obedience, we will draw near to Him. And as we're pursuing God, the Holy Spirit will shape our hearts by teaching and guiding us.

There's such an interesting cause and effect dynamic in our relationship with the Lord. The more I love God, the more I dislike my sinful nature. The more I love and appreciate Him, the more obeying becomes a natural outflow of my desire to be connected with Him. I love Him; therefore, I will obey.

In the end, righteousness does not come from doing right. True righteousness can only come from God because He has made us right through Christ. Turning away from the desires that capture our attention, whether they be sinful or noble, and turning towards God by desiring and pursuing Him above all else will lead to a flourishing and abundant life. It is here that we experience true freedom.

* * *

Questions for Reflection:

1. Read the following statements and identify which one is most reflective of your primary motive for obeying God's law and commandments:

    a. I obey because I tend to be a rule follower
    b. I obey out of duty and obligation
    c. I obey out of fear of being condemned by God
    d. I obey in the hopes of being rewarded/blessed by God
    e. I obey because I made a commitment to follow Christ
    f. My obedience is an expression of desiring and pursuing God

2. If authentic obedience is a natural result of our love for God, why do we tend to focus more on God's law and commandments instead of desiring and pursuing God?

3. In what ways do you allow morality (living out God's laws on your own) to get in the way of your identity in Christ (abiding in Him)?

4. Do you believe a righteous person is someone who "does right" or someone who is "made right"? Why?

5. How might understanding your identity in Christ help you in regards to obeying God?

9

KNOWING GOD:
TRUE RELATIONSHIP

*"This is eternal life, that they may know You, the only true God,
and Jesus Christ whom You have sent." John 17:3*

SEPTEMBER 2010

I'd been attending a DivorceCare group for a few months
at Worthington Christian Church. I felt so embarrassed
because there I was—a member of the church—seeking
help through one of our outreach programs. I hated the thought
of needing help, but the impending divorce overwhelmed me.
Life was going to be forever different and in a way that I'd never
anticipated or wanted. My American Dream of a wonderful
family who lived happily ever after had been shattered by divorce's
wrecking ball. Now I had to figure out my new normal and
how to care for Meredith as a single father.

The week's topic in my DivorceCare group was forgiveness—talk about a tough subject! How on earth was I going
to forgive Alyson when she was ending our relationship? Plus,
I didn't need to forgive Alyson for just one offense (leaving

our marriage), but I had to forgive her for multiple offences: breaking apart our family, emotionally wounding Meredith, and taking away half of Meredith's childhood from me because of our 50-50 shared parenting plan. I didn't know where to begin when it came to forgiving her or if I'd be able to do so.

I already knew what the Bible says about forgiveness, and the verse that troubled me most was Matthew 6:14-15: "For if you forgive others for their transgressions, your heavenly Father will also forgive you. But if you do not forgive others, then your Father will not forgive your transgressions." I knew it would be hypocritical if I claimed that Jesus forgave me, but I couldn't forgive her; I also knew God took forgiveness very seriously. But how could I possibly forgive the person who was closest in my life and had betrayed me? My discipline, motivation, and willpower were not going to be enough to forgive her because every ounce of my being wanted to hold all of these offences against her. I viewed the entire situation as a grave injustice because I was required to suffer the consequences of someone else's wrongdoing. But that's just one of the many ugly realities of sin—injustice thrives in the brokenness that sin creates.

As the DivorceCare session began, our facilitator handed each of us a clay brick paver. She told us to raise the brick over our heads with one hand and keep it raised until we finished watching the video on forgiveness. We all gave each other a bewildered look, wondering what this had to do with forgiveness. I think some of us were hoping we could use the brick to smash something; it'd be a therapeutic release of anger after the video was over! The video was only fifteen to twenty minutes long, but it was amazing how heavy that brick felt as the time passed. About halfway through the video, some people couldn't hold the brick above their heads any longer. Our facilitator told them to keep the brick raised and use their other arm for support if the fatigue was too much. After the video, our facilitator told us we could lower the brick. She then proceeded to ask how we felt, and all of us said we felt a tremendous amount of relief as soon as we put the brick down. She responded, "It's the same way with unforgiveness. At first, unforgiveness seems manageable and not that big of a deal. But over time, it will begin to break you down. Once you forgive someone, it will feel like a weight has been lifted, and you recognize how painful it was holding onto unforgiveness."

Here's the thing. I knew what the Bible said about forgiveness; I'd just participated in a physical demonstration of how forgiveness provides relief, and I'd learned the importance of it from my Divorce Care meeting. Still, I was having trouble forgiving Alyson, and I realized that I couldn't forgive her on my own—which is precisely where God wanted me.

* * *

Throughout my life, I've always enjoyed learning new things. Gaining knowledge and wisdom has always been a passion of mine, so studying my Bible became second nature. I usually studied a topic, theory, or question that interested me. I would go through periods where studying my Bible was a consistent daily routine like eating breakfast or brushing my teeth. At other times, I would go through periods of intense Bible study (multiple hours a day for several weeks) followed by hardly touching my Bible because I was exhausted from my mental workout that often left me more confused about a topic than when I first began studying it. One benefit from studying my Bible was that I knew a lot about God. Yet, with all of my knowledge about God, I lost sight of knowing Him relationally. Throughout most of my post-college life, I experienced a connection with Him from time to time, but this was usually for short periods and followed by long stretches of time where I felt disconnected from God.

My closest connection with God occurred shortly after I graduated college. I participated in a study called *Experiencing God* by Henry Blackaby and Claude King at Lane Avenue Baptist Church. This was an intense twelve-week study that focused on knowing and doing the will of God. During that short time, my faith grew more than at any other point in my life. I could truly say for the first time in my Christian journey I was being led by the Holy Spirit. That is to say, I was more interested in following God's way than my own. I was genuinely allowing the Lord to lead me where He wanted me to go, and in the process, I was experiencing God at a level of intimacy that I'd never experienced before. I not only learned what experiencing God meant, but I was also actively experiencing Him in my life. And I never wanted that connection to end.

This intimate connection to God and spiritual growth lasted for about a year after the study, and then it was almost as if God went silent. I couldn't figure out what was going on, and I desperately wanted His presence in my life. From that point, I took a very disciplined approach to my faith in the hopes of regaining the connection I'd once experienced. I figured if I wanted to experience Him more, I needed to read the Bible and pray more intently. But my attempts at rekindling this connection through studying my Bible and praying didn't seem to help. I couldn't figure out how to transition from knowing about God to knowing God, which left me confused and frustrated. It wasn't until God put me in a position where I had to totally depend on Him to forgive Alyson that I learned what it takes to transition from understanding God intellectually to knowing God relationally.

Knowing Others: Using the Head and the Heart

The first step in any relationship is to understand basic information about the other person such as their values, beliefs, interests, and desires. Once we know this, we make a decision to engage in the relationship or move on. If we decide to establish a relationship, the degree to which the relationship grows depends on two factors: an intellectual understanding of the person and a relational connection to the person. Both of these must be present in order for an intimate, authentic, and healthy relationship to exist.

In our advanced digital age of information, we have knowledge at our fingertips—something no other generation has encountered. But while we can quickly know a lot about people, we don't *really* know them. The failure to truly know someone creates a false sense of connection. Take our American president for example. Virtually every American knows President Donald Trump, but the vast majority of Americans possess only an intellectual understanding of him. No matter how much a person knows about President Trump, no relationship exists unless that person and the President are connected relationally. And both must desire a relationship in order for a relational connection to exist. Mere intellectual knowledge about a person does not mean a relationship exists.

Likewise, a person cannot experience an intimate, authentic, and healthy relationship simply through a relational connection only. A relational connection to a person absent of intellectual knowledge is nothing but infatuation. Here, people can enter into a relationship without knowing anything about the other person and expose themselves to a host of dangerous situations such as being used, abused, and betrayed. Both intellectual knowledge about a person and a relational connection are required for a healthy relationship to exist, and no relationship exists if one is expressed without the other. Additionally, a healthy relational connection can only grow to the extent of our intellectual understanding of the other person. As we grow in our understanding of a person and draw close relationally, only then can we say that we truly know that person.

KNOWING GOD

This same principle is true of our relationship with God. As He reveals Himself to us, His Word teaches us about His character, and we gain an intellectual understanding of God. For instance, through Scripture we learn that God is holy and loving, He pursues His people, and He is faithful to them. After we gain a basic understanding of who God is and what He's done for us, we then make a decision whether or not to commit to following Him all the days of our life. This commitment is represented by a single event in time when a person is spiritually born again and sealed forever with the Holy Spirit. Afterwards, our commitment to Him continues to grow as we allow God to reveal Himself to us, and we abide in Him. This commitment represents the eternal life that is found in knowing God.

It's interesting that in order to know God relationally, we must first come to an understanding of who He is. Of course, we will never be able to *fully* comprehend the depths of God with our minuscule, finite minds. If anyone says they must completely understand God before they believe, they will never become a Christian. At some point, they need to take a step of faith and believe that God is who He says He is. Unfortunately, many intellectuals get hung up on this very point. They seem to hold on to the thought that they must first understand how God works before they can believe; however, this type of logic isn't what governs our daily lives. For example, I don't have to understand how an air conditioner works to believe that one will keep me cool in the summer. I don't have to understand how a car works in order to believe that one will move me from point A to point B more quickly than if I walked. So, why would I need to completely understand God before I believe in Him?

THE INTELLECT ALONE: HOW AMERICAN PHARISEES UNDERSTAND GOD

American Pharisees claim they know God, but what they usually mean is they know *about* God. They know their Bibles very well, and they understand the promises and truths contained within it. They understand the concepts of justification, sanctification, grace, mercy, love, atonement, sacrifice, and forgiveness. They acknowledge Biblical truths such as the Triune God, Virgin birth, and Christ's death and resurrection. They also comprehend that all Scripture is the inerrant Word of God. They know all about the miracles and can explain them in amazing detail. Yet when pressed, they will admit their relationship with God seems distant and cold. They might be inspired from time to time by what they read in the Bible, but most of the time, they feel very little connection with God even though they know a lot about Him.

The Pharisees in Jesus' day held a strikingly similar position to the modern-day American Pharisee. Jesus described these people as, "Whitewashed tombs which appear beautiful on the outside, but on the inside, they are filled with dead man's bones and all uncleanness." Jesus was basically saying that they looked good on the outside, but their insides (their heart and character) lacked the same beauty. He went on to say that they appeared as "Righteous to men, but inwardly are full of hypocrisy and lawlessness" (Matthew 23:27-28). So, while the Pharisees were considered experts in religious matters and held tightly to the Law, Jesus said they were as good as dead with no righteousness in them. Why? They were more interested in appearing righteous than receiving the true-life transformation that only God could provide.

THE NECESSITY OF THE HEART

If we try to understand God from purely an academic, intellectual standpoint, we will naturally gravitate toward our own interpretation of God's Word instead of allowing His Word to change us. Under this approach, we will never know Him relationally because we are trying to figure Him out based on our own knowledge and understanding (Proverbs 3:5-6). If we really want to know God, He must reveal Himself to us through His written Word, and we must allow His Word to penetrate our hearts through humility, surrender, and obedience. It is one thing to say, "I'm going to do my best to understand what the Bible says" and completely another to say, "I can't possibly know anything about God unless He reveals Himself to me through His Word." The former implies the reader is in control and will interpret what is read in the Bible. The latter says that God is in control. As such, the reader surrenders control so that God may speak into the individual's life through the Holy Spirit.

If we only focus on head knowledge about God, then we completely miss out on the relationship. We may know a lot about God, but we experience emptiness in our relationship with Him. That is why we need to focus not only on understanding God, but also on knowing God relationally. As we focus on growing our relationship with Him, then we will experience God *both* intellectually and relationally. This table distinguishes between understanding God and knowing Him relationally.

Table 1

Understanding God Intellectually	Knowing God Relationally
Learns about God	Loves God
Comes from the Head	Comes from the Heart
Aware of God	Connected to God
Explains God	Experiences God
Possesses information concerning God	Possesses intimacy with God
State of doing (research/study/serve)	State of being (presence/companionship)
Demonstrates dependence on self	Demonstrates dependence on God
Established in the mind	Established in the heart
Draws conclusions about God	Gets lost in the wonder of God
Requires no faith	Requires faith

American Pharisees are comfortable focusing on intellectual knowledge for the simple reason that they are in control. They can measure their spiritual progress by the number of minutes spent reading the Bible, the number of verses memorized, or the amount of theological arguments won. Yet very little spiritual transformation actually occurs because the heart is forgotten in the intellectual process. Being disciplined about studying the Bible and learning about God might make people more educated, but it does very little in terms of life transformation if they don't allow God's Word to penetrate their hearts. Heart change will not occur until we take what we've studied in the Bible, accept it as truth, and integrate that truth into our daily lives. As we do this, our faith will grow. No faith is required to study the Bible and learn about God, but great faith is required to allow God to change our hearts and to act upon Biblical truths.

Measuring progress in knowing God relationally is a lot more abstract. We cannot use rulers, scales, or task lists to determine our connectedness with God. However, the Scriptures are clear that our relationship with God will grow by the measure we allow God's Word to transform our hearts. This transformation begins with hearing God's Word (Romans 10:17). If we are not reading the Bible on a consistent basis and allowing it to transform our minds and hearts, then we should expect very little faith in return. For faith to grow, we must (1) understand God's Word, (2) claim it to be true, and (3) depend on God's Word by living out that which we claim to be true. If we don't act upon it, then we don't believe it regardless of what we proclaim. American Pharisees tend to focus on the intellect only; the desire is to understand God's Word and stop there. They claim they believe it to be true, but they do not rely upon God's Word as if their lives depended on it.

> HEART CHANGE WILL NOT OCCUR UNTIL WE TAKE WHAT WE'VE STUDIED IN THE BIBLE, ACCEPT IT AS TRUTH, AND INTEGRATE THAT TRUTH INTO OUR DAILY LIVES.

THE HEAD AND THE HEART: THE FOUNDATION OF TRUE WORSHIP

When we act upon the truths God has revealed because we understand with our heads and also believe in our hearts, we suddenly experience a sacrificial commitment to God. We now have the ability to give up our ambitions and trade them in for God's plan, and our faith is no longer about our needs and our wants. We engage in planned suffering and submit ourselves to the Lord, and this is the place where we begin to truly worship Him. In his 2013 best-selling book *Gods at War*, author Kyle Idleman provides the following insight concerning worship:

> Worship is the built-in human reflex to put your hope in something or someone and then chase after it. You hold something up and then give your life to pursue it. If you live in this world, then sooner or later you grow some assumptions concerning what life is all about, what you should be going after. And when you begin to align your life with that pursuit, then, whether you realize it or not, you are worshiping.

Based on Kyle's definition of worship, I was worshiping almost everything else but God in my days as an American Pharisee. Even though anyone who knew me would have said I was a devoted man of God, they were basing their conclusion merely on external actions and behaviors. While I lived a very virtuous and disciplined life, my heart was full of hypocrisy. My worship was devoted to the things that made my life easier, more pleasant, and more secure. I found my identity in my career, my value in my family, and my righteousness in my conduct. I knew that I was saved by God's grace, but

I didn't see much value in my salvation while I was here on earth. So, my relationship with God was reduced to participating in the typical Christian disciplines to show God that I was devoted to Him in the hopes He would reward me with the material blessings of my American Dream. I claimed to be worshiping God, but I was really committing idolatry by preferring comfort over Christ.

Deep down, I knew I wanted to experience a closer relationship with God, but I was more focused on my own life than the life God had designed for me. Instead of knowing Him relationally, I settled for knowing Him intellectually. Learning about God was much more convenient and manageable. I got to choose what to study, when to fit it into my schedule, and how to integrate what I learned into my life.

THE FREEDOM OF FORGIVENESS: HOW DO WE GET IT?

When I was faced with forgiving Alyson, I was holding onto the American Pharisee view that it's up to the individual to muster up enough effort and willpower to obey God's commands—forgiving others was no different. For most of my adult life, I'd been able to muscle through my faith using self-discipline, motivation, and focus. But now, I was faced head on with something I knew didn't exist within me—the ability to forgive Alyson. The emotional wound of betrayal runs deep, and it doesn't get any deeper than the betrayal of a spouse.

Knowing I was unable to forgive Alyson on my own, I turned to God in desperation. Suddenly, my heart became very engaged in my faith. I confessed to Him that I couldn't forgive her on my own. I just couldn't shake the thought that what she did to me was wrong. She broke the covenant of our marriage, and I wanted some sort of justice. So, I asked God to give me the strength to forgive because I knew forgiving her was part of His plan. I also recognized that unforgiveness only hurts me because I become hostage to the wrongs committed against me. Even more, I knew that unforgiveness could never pay the penalty of the sin that was committed. It was just a prison that would ultimately enslave me because I wasn't letting go of the wrongdoing.

Our hunger to keep record of the wrongs committed against us stems from the original sin of eating from the tree of the knowledge of good and evil. Man was never supposed to eat from that tree, but in that one act of disobedience, our minds became opened to something they never should have known: the knowledge of good and evil. That's why our natural reaction to a wrong committed against us is to hold the wrongdoing against the other person. But here's the problem: while the original sin of "knowing good and evil" makes us aware that a wrong has been committed against us, we are also incapable of making restitution because we aren't God. Therefore, we can't seek justice in a way that reconciles the wrong committed against us. Governments can create prudent judicial institutions that administer punitive damages for civil or criminal offenses. But even the most noble of human governments will always fall short of healing the victim's pain from the wrong committed against them. Just as we were never designed to know good and evil, we were also never designed to seek retribution for the wrongs committed against us. God is the only one who is capable of exercising justice so that it remains in perfect balance with His holiness, wrath, grace, anger, mercy, vengeance, and love.

If we seek vengeance on our own, we displace God's supremacy by exercising our own will over His authority. Our inherent brokenness of thinking we are like God will begin to convince us that we know better than God. Thus, if justice isn't playing out the way we want, then we believe God is withholding something good from us, and we seek vengeance on our own terms. Once again, our pride blocks God's grace, and God opposes this prideful behavior. Coming to terms with the fact that unforgiveness causes us to hope for a better past or better outcome can be very difficult. Until we recognize this, we are left wallowing in the pit of unforgiveness because our pride doesn't want to let go.

One of the greatest gifts God has given mankind is the ability to forgive themselves and others. Without this gift, people would be left holding onto every wrong they have ever committed and every wrong committed against them. Withholding forgiveness causes us to live our lives in sorrow, anger, or bitterness because we are holding on to the wrongs done to us. In fact, unforgiveness gives even more power to the perpetrator because we continue to live with the pain of what was done to us. That's the strange irony—with unforgiveness, victims are required to hold onto the offences committed against them. In order for me to continue to hold an offense *against* my perpetrator, I am required to hold *onto* the offense myself. So as long as I fail to forgive, I will also bear the weight of the transgression. Forgiveness is the antidote to guilt, shame, and injustice that results from the wrongs we commit and the wrongs committed against us.

Receiving the Strength to Forgive

If you are struggling with unforgiveness (or anything else), remember that you can know God relationally by humbly submitting that very trial before Him. When we are at our weakest is when we experience God's strength working in and through us. The Lord's promise to the Apostle Paul is the same promise He makes to us: "My grace is sufficient for you, for My power is made perfect in weakness" (II Corinthians 12:9).

God tells us to forgive others not as an arbitrary command, but out of real intention and purpose. Forgiving sets us free from the bondage of the offense. Forgiveness can be tough, and sometimes it can seem impossible. Still, we have the opportunity to know God on a personal level in those very moments of impossibility. When we experience Him transforming our hearts, we become able to do the impossible and our faith will grow. Through this transformation, we will know God relationally through personal connection and receive the privilege of experiencing eternal life with Him before reaching Heaven.

It wasn't until I had to rely upon Him for the strength to forgive Alyson that my relational connection with God began to grow. I knew I wasn't capable of forgiving her on my own, so I had to put my hope in God alone to take me through this process. My heart pursued Him because I knew that only God could overcome this obstacle within me. For the first time in a very long time, I worshiped God for who He was—the One who has ability and strength far beyond my human capability—and I saw the value of Him transforming my heart into one that could forgive Alyson. Through this painful experience, I was being transformed into the image of His likeness, and I began to know God relationally once again.

* * *

Questions for Reflection:

1. In what ways have you been focused more on knowing about God intellectually than knowing God relationally?

2. How does knowing God relationally allow you to experience healing from an emotional wound?

3. Are you holding onto unforgiveness? If so, are you allowing it to create a barrier in your relationship with God or are you willing to ask God to help you to forgive your perpetrator?

10

RIGHT VIEW OF GOD: TRUE PERSPECTIVE

"That men may know from the rising to the setting of the sun that there is no one besides Me. I am the Lord, and there is no other, the One forming light and creating darkness, causing well-being and creating calamity; I am the Lord who does all these."
Isaiah 45:6-7

"The Son is the image of the invisible God, the firstborn over all creation. For by Him all things were created, both in the heavens and on earth, visible and invisible, whether thrones or dominions or rulers or authorities, all things have been created through Him and for Him." Colossians 1:15-17

JULY 5, 2015 (JOURNAL ENTRY)

*T*omorrow is our first official day on site with our missionary partner IsleGo. We went on a trip this afternoon to see the two sites where we are going to build homes for the local residents. It is a very impoverished area called "The Bush." We took a bus to a drop off point and hiked about a quarter mile where homes are scattered around *a woodsy hill that overlooks the ocean. When facing the ocean, it has a spectacular view—a place where people would build mansions. But when I look away from the ocean and focus on the surroundings, I noticed I was standing in the middle of extreme poverty. The houses are about the size of a shed—much smaller than my kitchen at home. There are a lot of goats, dogs, and trash. Fortunately, the goats and dogs are tied up, and we've been instructed to not even touch them because of the diseases they carry. Most of the homes don't have glass windows or a door, just curtains to cover the openings. Most of the properties are extremely cluttered, but some owners keep up their homes and want them to be presentable. Yet, something seems strange to me: scattered amongst the very poor were very expensive homes. It appeared as though no distinction existed between the rich and poor as it does in America.*

We've been told the neighborhood we are working in is safe during the day, but after the sun goes down, the local police refuse to patrol the area because of extreme violence. Our lodging facilities are located in a nearby town that is much safer. But even our facility is well-fortified with armed guards, bars, and gates. We've been instructed to travel in groups of no less than three and at least one male must be present at all times. Each villa within our facility comes equipped with metal bars across all the doors and windows. It usually takes me about fifteen minutes just to lock up for the night and unlock in the morning. Due to the security measures our mission team is taking, I feel very safe, but I also recognize I'm not in southern Delaware County Ohio any longer.

I'm scheduled to facilitate our mission team's devotion tonight and plan on discussing the following verses:

"No one can come to me unless the Father who sent Me draws him; and I will raise him up on the last day" (John 6:44).

"But you will receive power when the Holy Spirit has come upon you, and you shall be my witnesses both in Jerusalem and in all Judea and Samaria and even to the remotest part of the earth" (Acts 1:6-8)

"For we cannot stop speaking about what we have seen and heard" (Acts 4:20).

I also plan on sharing with our team an Adrian Rogers quote: "Jesus didn't say, You shall be my lawyers. Jesus said, 'You shall be my witnesses.' A lawyer argues a case, but Jesus says we are called to be a witness—to tell what we've seen and heard."[6] Those who are blind spiritually are unable to see things the way God's children see them, so it is futile and a waste of energy to argue and debate spiritual matters with those who are spiritually blind. When we tell others what we have "seen and heard," we need to be aware that some truly can't understand what we are talking about. Thus, our job is to witness, not judge others or defend our position.

Words can't express my joy and excitement to be a part of God's kingdom work through this mission trip. When I reflect back on last year and how I almost died from my pulmonary embolism, I am so grateful that God has graciously given me more time on earth. Obeying God's calling for me to go on the mission trip to Jamaica last year literally saved my life, even though, in the end, I couldn't make it. Now, I get to experience the Jamaican people, culture, and land a year later, completely healed from my embolism. I always understood that God is good all of the time, but now I have come to know His goodness through experiencing Him actively working in my life. I used to possess such a distorted view of God, but now I can sense that He is taking off my blinders so I can see Him for who He is. I seem to be coming into a right view of Him.

* * *

One day soon after I'd returned from my first mission trip to Jamaica, I was flipping around radio stations in my truck, and I came across a James MacDonald broadcast where he made the following statement: "A wrong view of God leads to wrong thinking and attitudes, which is what leads to wrong behavior."[7] This one statement has had a tremendous influence on my faith walk and helped me recognize the reality that what I do is a product of what I believe and not necessarily what I intellectually know to be true. Often, I'll notice a behavior in my life that is not consistent with who God is. This happens because my thinking about God is distorted, and therefore my actions reflect it. Here are just a few examples from everyday life where I reveal a distorted view of God:

- Behavior: Worry

  o Wrong thinking about God: He is not in control
  o Incorrect view of God: He is not omnipotent

- Behavior: Pursuit of my own ambitions

  o Wrong thinking about God: I know what's best for me more than God does
  o Incorrect view of God: He is not omniscient

- Behavior: Live a virtuous life with the hope of being blessed

  o Wrong thinking about God: He shows special favor to those who obey Him
  o Incorrect view of God: His love is conditional

- Behavior: Unforgiveness

  o Wrong thinking about God: He will let my perpetrator off the hook

- o   Incorrect view of God: He is not just

- Behavior: Sin

  - o   Wrong thinking about God: He is withholding something good from me
  - o   Incorrect view of God: He is not good

Unfortunately, the list goes on, and I'm disappointed that my view of God is often so distorted. Ironically, if someone asked me if I thought God was sovereign, omnipotent, omniscient, good, just, and unconditionally loving, I would respond with absolute assurance, "Of course, I believe these truths about God." But if I really believed these truths, then my daily behavior would reflect it, and I would:

- Never worry or sin

- Always rest in His grace instead of trying to per-form in the hopes of winning favor

- Always forgive without hesitation

- Always prioritize His will over my agenda

WHO GOD REALLY IS

The Bible teaches that God is all-powerful, all-knowing, and self-existent. His character and essence are perfect in every way and never change. He is not limited in any way. He has no beginning or end and is not bound by time or space. He is the definition and standard of what it means to be faithful, good, just, merciful, gracious, loving, and holy. We are unable to hide from His presence or act outside of His absolute sovereignty. And no one will ever come close to fully understanding Him because of His infinite nature. He is One Triune God of Father, Son, and Holy Spirit. Nothing has pre-existed God, and nothing will ever outlast God. With mere words, God spoke galaxies into existence and created them out of nothing.

God exercises absolute sovereignty irrespective of man's free choice, and He orchestrates His rule, governance, and control in a way that ultimately accomplishes His perfect plan of redeeming this broken world and reconciling His children to Himself through Jesus Christ. We can choose to rebel against God's plan and to reject God Himself, but our rebellion and denial of God will not thwart His plan. Before time began, He took into account all of our mistakes, shortfalls, and unbelief, so that His plan would ultimately prevail irrespective of man's will. As a matter of fact, He has already determined the goal of His plan even before all things were created. This truth is difficult for our minds to fathom because we are tiny, weak finite humans who are limited by time and space, and God transcends time and space. He is the Author of all things including mankind. His eternal nature and omnipotence allow Him to see how all things work together for His good and His glory. Simply put—God's plan will be accomplished with or without you and me. This is the God of all creation, and we have the privilege of worshipping Him for all of eternity.

THE ORIGIN OF OUR DISTORTED VIEW

Much of my distorted view of God can be traced back to the false belief that God is only marginally bigger than I am. I may acknowledge that He is greater than me, but deep down, in the recesses of my brokenness, I only want

Him to be just a *little* bigger than me, so I can challenge Him on matters I don't agree with. I want a safe God—One who acts, behaves, and rationalizes moral and ethical situations just as I would.

When we are presented with a truth about God yet experience something that our finite minds believe contradicts that truth, then we begin to doubt God. We ask ourselves questions such as:

If God is loving, why would He...
If God is just, why would He...
If God is merciful, why would He...
If God knows all things, why doesn't He...

These questions reveal much about our distorted view of God. We believe that we possess enough wisdom to argue against God's judgment. We convince ourselves that God sometimes makes mistakes, and therefore we begin to doubt His sovereignty, providence, omniscience, love, holiness, mercy, and wisdom. And what we've effectively done is replaced the God of the Bible with a manufactured god created by our own knowledge, wisdom, and intellect.

The problem with creating our own god is that this god will eventually disappoint. When we attempt to understand God based on our own pursuit of the truth, we limit God through human reason and logic. We fail to leave any room for God to be God and for us to be mere mortal beings. Instead, the created manufactures his own god based on his own understanding. In most every case, this manufactured god becomes a reflection of the person who created it. And in a strange irony, the created become trapped within their own brokenness by worshiping themselves.

Whether we like it or not, the truth is we will never be able to fully comprehend God simply because our finite minds cannot contain The Infinite God. The created can never be greater than the Creator. To claim we can fully comprehend God is to claim foolishness. A God we can't comprehend may frustrate us from time to time, but He will always provide our spiritual hearts with amazement, wonder, and an understanding that we are infinitely smaller than the One who created us.

THE ROLE OF HUMILITY

So, how do we fix our view of God? Ironically, we can't. It's impossible for us to obtain a right view of God on our own. Yet our culture tells us something contrary to this truth. We are constantly bombarded with motivational quotes that tell us we can do anything we set our minds to. We control our destiny, and all we have to do is pull ourselves up by the bootstraps and get to work. We need to make things happen or nothing will get done right. It is up to us if we want to experience a healthy, prosperous, and successful life. American Pharisees buy into this philosophy and begin applying it to various aspects of their lives where it doesn't belong. They quickly take this approach to life, see that it works well, and attempt to replicate this same philosophy in their spiritual lives. They are misguided into thinking that they can initiate spiritual growth or gain a right view of God independently of Him.

The Bible provides a sharp contrast to what the world tells us. God's Word says our hearts are deceitful and desperately sick (Jeremiah 17:9), and no one seeks after God (Romans 3:11). Thus, all of my human efforts of explaining God, justifying God, and living according to

God's commands are simply this—flawed human efforts. And the Bible is clear that all of our virtuous deeds are nothing but filthy rags to God (Isaiah 64:6). The fact that any of us has even the slightest interest at all to inquire about God is a testimony of God's desire to reveal Himself to us, and it has *nothing* to do with us. Every time I reach out to God with pure motives, it is a direct result of His perfect unconditional love for me. Every time I respond positively to a truth about God, it's because He's revealing Himself to me. It is God who is good—not us.

What must we do? We must humble ourselves before God in prayer and ask Him to reveal Himself to us through His Word, so we might gain a right view of Him. Once we recognize that pride is negatively affecting our relationship with God, we can bring this before God by confessing our pride and asking Him to create a pure heart within us. In doing so, we will experience Him working in our lives firsthand. We see this example set before us in Psalm 143:10, when David asks God to teach him how to do His will. David clearly recognized that he didn't have the knowledge or ability to do God's will based upon his own understanding.

Our pastor at Lifepoint Church, Dean Fulks, describes pride as, "The arrogant refusal to let God be God."[8] Every one of us, whether we are a believer or not, will be tempted to go through life using our own knowledge, ability, and effort to advance our agenda. Regardless of whether our agenda is corrupt or virtuous, the problem is we prefer our own view rather than adjusting to God's. As such, we fail to let God be God if we don't allow Him to rule our lives. We resort to relying on our own strength to get through life, and it is a life devoid of the very strength that God is willing to freely give us if we humble ourselves before Him.

Humility begins with understanding the chasm between how small we are and how majestic God really is; it is in humility that our lives will change. The more we become aware of God's majesty, the bigger He becomes and the more we recognize just how small and insignificant we really are. The bigger God becomes, the humbler we become. We stop drawing our own conclusions about God and allow Him to speak into our lives. We come into a right view of God, and our behaviors align with the truth. This is the essence of heart transformation.

GAINING CLARITY OF PURPOSE

In my days of living as an American Pharisee, most of my prayers came from a prideful attitude that significantly limited my view of God. My prayers were full of self-serving requests for the things I wanted. I hardly ever prayed with an attitude of seeking God's will and aligning myself to His plan. The "Me Gospel" distorted my view of God because I mistakenly thought I needed God to get me through life without any hardship. I viewed the Scriptures in such a way that would ultimately benefit me and then aligned my prayer life to this agenda.

Here are just a few examples of verses I used to rationalize my own agenda:

- *"I can do all things through Him who strengthens me" (Philippians 4:13).*

  I used this verse to motivate me in pursuing my own agenda. I recall telling myself, "All I need to do is press on, achieve, succeed. The work will be worth it in the long run. God helps those who help themselves, and He will see all of the hard work

I am doing to provide a nice life for Alyson and Meredith." I told myself that I wasn't committing any overt sins or hurting anyone, so there wasn't any harm in praying for material prosperity and success.

- *"If you ask the Father anything in My name, He will give it to you" (John 16:23).*

I prayed for every opportunity to be promoted at work, for every pay raise, and for every advancement in the good and nice life.

- *"'For I know the plans that I have for you,' declares the Lord, 'plans for welfare and not for calamity to give you a future and a hope" (Jeremiah 29:11).*

I defined welfare in worldly terms, so I prayed for material prosperity and a happily ever after fairy tale ending to my life here on earth.

My self-centered, self-motivated, and self-serving view of the Gospel elevated me over God, and I followed the "Me Gospel" instead of the true Gospel. This "Me Gospel" distorted my view of what it meant to be a committed Christ-follower. I wanted God to get me through life unscathed, so I could finally get to Heaven and continue enjoying life for all eternity. I wanted *my* kingdom come and *my* will to be done, here on earth as it is in Heaven.

After God humbled me and revealed that I was an American Pharisee who pursued the "Me Gospel," I began to change my approach to the Scriptures and prayer. I began approaching God's Word and prayer in humility and surrender. I confessed that I couldn't know anything about God unless He revealed Himself to me through His Word. I no longer took an academic approach to figuring Him out, and I stopped making petty requests that only benefited my agenda. My prayer time changed and reflected, for the first time, the following:

Being in awe of God and being still in His presence: 40% of my prayer time

Giving Thanks to God: 25% of my prayer time

Praying for others: 25% of my prayer time

Confessing sin: 5% of my prayer time

Personal requests: less than 5% of my prayer time

Please note that the time breakdown is illustrative—I don't fall into the trap of my former American Pharisee days where I would be tempted to time myself to make sure I was spending the right amount of time on each topic. Also, my personal requests are no longer about how to increase *my* kingdom but, rather, are personal requests for opportunities to participate in His Kingdom work. Obviously, I still have the occasional requests that I bring forth in prayer, but the difference now is that my requests are not my primary motivation for prayer. My main motivation for prayer is to simply be in His presence, to cease striving, and to know that He is God.

THE POWER OF PRAYER

Shortly after my prayer life changed, I began seeing a change in how I viewed God. And when I used my prayer time to pray God's Word back to Him, my spiritual growth jumped off the charts! I discovered that His Word became my word when I prayed the Scriptures, and I began to have a right view of God. Taking God's Word and personalizing it in prayer has radically transformed my heart. Instead of constantly making personal requests to God, I'm aligning myself to His Word and surrendering my own agenda, thoughts, and conclusions about what is best for me. I'm allowing His written Word to penetrate my heart, change my life, and compel me to take real steps of faith. Consequently, I no longer desire the American Pharisee lifestyle of pursuing the "Me Gospel", because I am gaining a right view of God as He reveals Himself to me through prayer.

Like the apostle Paul, who was once a Pharisee himself, I have turned away from my old way of living where I pursued my own agenda while claiming to be a Christ follower. Now, I am all in for Christ, and everything I do is founded upon my relationship with Him. In my old life, I used to claim this truth, but my life reflected something different. I viewed my relationship with Christ as just one of many aspects of my life. But now, my relationship with Christ is the **foundation** of every other aspect of my life. I am far from perfect and still struggle with the old ghosts that creep back into my way of thinking. I am surely doomed to falling back into the American Pharisee lifestyle as soon as I begin believing I have the Christian life all figured out. It is for this very reason that I must take up my cross and deny myself **daily** if I want to be a committed follower of Christ. As Paul states in Romans, I am a living sacrifice, and the problem with being a living sacrifice is that I can run from the altar at any given time. As I proceed through my Christian journey in humility, surrender, and obedience, I now pray back to God in my own words what Paul wrote in Philippians 3:7-14:

Whatever things I considered gain to create the American Dream, those things I have counted as loss for the sake of Christ. More than that, I count all of my worldly success in Corporate America to be loss in view of the surpassing value of knowing Christ Jesus as my Lord, for whom I have suffered the loss of my "good and nice life," and count it but rubbish so that I may gain Christ, and may be found in Him not having a righteousness of my own derived from my own interpretation of what the Bible says, but rather a righteousness established as my identity which is through a saving faith in Christ. A righteousness which comes from God on the basis of faith, that I may know Him relationally and the power of His resurrection that gives eternal life and the fellowship of His sufferings in His Kingdom work here on earth, being conformed to His death; in order that I may attain to the resurrection from the dead. Not that I have already obtained Christ-likeness or have already become perfect, but I press on so that I may lay hold of His purpose for me for which Christ has also chosen me. I have not laid hold of it yet; but one thing I do; forgetting my past and reaching forward to what lies ahead, I press on toward the goal for the prize of the upward call of God in Christ Jesus.

There is nothing special about the words of this prayer. The power comes from the truth of God's promises and an authentic humble heart that responds favorably to the truth He's revealed to me.

There used to be a day when I completely understood Paul's words in Philippians 3, but I didn't really believe them in my heart. Honestly, Paul's declaration used to be quite disturbing to me. I couldn't figure out why he would be willing to throw away everything he once knew and trade it in for a life plagued with suffering for the sake of Christ. I intellectually knew the right answer was that I must possess the same attitude as Paul and, as such, would confess that Jesus was the top priority in my life. But deep down, I believed that the goal here on earth was to get through life with as little discomfort as possible. Certainly, planned suffering was not on my agenda for growing spiritually. I demonstrated my loyalty to God by tithing, serving, consistently reading my Bible, and praying regularly. The problem with this approach was the fact that I was in control. For example, even though I gave 10% of my income regularly, I gave out of my abundance; I didn't give generously. Similarly, I determined how I wanted to serve and when it was convenient; I wasn't really a servant at all.

A GENEROUS SERVANT

The mission trip to Jamaica in the summer of 2015 was my first mission trip, and it was life-changing. Part of this life-changing experience was the fact that I should have died a year earlier, but God had spared my life. I now see each day as a gift and not an entitlement. I also had the experience of sharing the Gospel with the nations by visiting a small community near St. Ann's Bay, Jamaica. As an upper class white-collar American, I understood that I possessed certain privileges that most people around the world didn't, but I never really understood the degree of disparity between the rich and poor until Jamaica. The majority of Americans who travel to Jamaica only see it from their luxury cruise liner or lush resort. They see a tropical paradise and vacation destination to relax and recharge from the hustle and bustle of American life. Most tourists would be shocked to see how the majority of local Jamaicans live on a daily basis. Sadly, many tourists don't even care.

One night during our mission trip, our leader, Bryan, provided some interesting statistics about affluence that he'd learned from the website, irememberthepoor.org:

- A person with non-cash assets of $2,200 ranks in the top 50% of the world's wealthiest individuals

- A person who earns $1,500 or more annually is in the top 20% of the world's income earners

- A person who earns $25,000 or more annually is in the top 10% of the world's income earners

- A person who earns $50,000 or more annually is in the top 1% of the world's income earners

- A person who has sufficient food, decent clothes, lives in a house or apartment, and has a reasonably reliable means of transportation, is in the top 15% of the world's wealthiest people[9]

Bryan then challenged us with this statement:

> In light of these statistics, what you have seen here in Jamaica, and knowing that both the rich and poor are equally valued by God, why do you believe God has provided us with so much wealth? What are you doing with your wealth?

His challenge was not intended to give us a guilt trip or make us feel rotten about ourselves. It was a genuine call to reflect on something serious that, quite frankly, we Americans take for granted. I knew money wasn't the source of happiness and didn't fix every problem, but my actions reflected the opposite. And now, I was brought face to face with a reality that made me uncomfortable. I knew by these statistics that I was extremely rich, and yet I capped my charitable giving to a measly 10% of what I earned. Why? Because I took a legalistic approach to tithing. I figured as long as I gave 10% of my earnings, I was doing what was required of me. But now, I recognize that if I possess a true love for God and a desire to participate in His kingdom work here on earth, then 10% of what I earn is the bare minimum of what I should be giving financially to further God's kingdom. It's not that God needs our money; His will, will be done with or without our money. We give because money has such a grip on us, and we need to constantly remind ourselves that God is our provider—not our money. In our American tradition of independence, we depend a little too much on ourselves and depend too little on God. Self-sufficiency is a good thing, but we Americans have made it a god-thing by elevating our independence above God Himself.

> SELF-SUFFICIENCY IS A GOOD THING, BUT WE AMERICANS HAVE MADE IT A GOD-THING BY ELEVATING OUR INDEPENDENCE ABOVE GOD HIMSELF.

Americans idolize affluence, and American Pharisees commit adultery against their relationship with God when they pursue financial freedom over pursuing God.

So, how does an American Pharisee turn away from idolizing money? Give until it hurts, and then give some more. Smashing the idols we've come to depend on for so long is not easy, and it will be painful. But the rewards for turning away from false gods and worshiping the true God are priceless. God used a near-death experience, a short-term mission trip to Jamaica, and Bryan to break me free from the bondage that the love of money had on my heart. I have been so grateful for those moments, and my gratefulness has translated into heart-felt generosity. Instead of giving and serving, I am now a generous servant. As my generosity has grown, so has my desire for the nations to hear the Gospel.

By God's grace, I now live in humility, viewing others as more important than me. I have become a generous servant for God's kingdom work. My life of humility stems from a right view of God, and my thinking is now aligned to some basic truths: He is big, and I am small. He is strong, and I am weak. He is omniscient, and I am foolish. He is sovereign, and I am His subject. He is God, and I am not.

I can now view life from an eternal perspective, and I'm much less interested in what this world has to offer me. He has begun showing me the world as He sees it, and I'm seeing things from an eternal perspective instead of a temporary one. I eagerly look to pass His blessings on to others with excitement and enthusiasm. If I'm lucky, I only have another thirty or forty years here on earth. Until my time comes, my prayer is to be a blessing to others instead of being blessed.

As I draw near to God in His righteousness and holiness, I become acutely aware of my own sinfulness, inadequacy, and flaws. As I draw near to God in His sovereignty, I grow more fearful of Him. As I grow closer to God in His majesty, I realize that I know very little about Him and possess very few answers. It is only by the blood of Christ that I continue to proceed in awe of Him. As I draw near to God in His mercy, I grow more grateful of Him. As I draw near His grace, I grow more thankful for Him. And as I draw near to God in His love, I begin to see the world as He sees it. I grow in compassion for my fellow man, wanting for him what I've already received—forgiveness, healing, and the true freedom to live a life glorifying God and enjoying Him. It is a privilege to be connected with His kingdom building work here on earth. And that alone motivates me to share the good news of the redeeming love of Christ.

* * *

Questions for Reflection:

1. Identify some behaviors in your life that contradict what it means to follow Christ. How do these behaviors reveal an incorrect thinking about God? How does this translate to an incorrect view of God?

2. How might confessing these misconceptions about God and asking Him to give you a right view of Him begin to change your behaviors? Is this something you are willing to do? Why or why not?

3. In what ways does money have a grip on you? Do you have a tendency to prefer money and financial status over God? How might you begin breaking free from this bondage?

11

PURSUIT OF GOD: #BLESSED

"For where your treasure is, there your heart will be also."
Luke 12:34

"Delight yourself in the Lord; and He will give you the desires of your heart. Commit your way to the Lord, trust also in Him, and He will do it. He will bring forth your righteousness as the light and your judgment as the noonday. Rest in the Lord and wait patiently for Him."
Psalms 37:4-7

FEBRUARY 17, 2013

I t was midmorning, and I was alone in the house. Nervousness consumed me; I couldn't stop pacing around the great room, and fear gradually crept into my mind. I knew my life was going to change from that day forward, but wasn't sure I was ready. I tried to divert my attention by doing a workout in my basement gym, but after every set of weights, my mind immediately drifted back to the upcoming events that were to take place that afternoon. It seemed as though *almost every possible emotion flooded my mind: from delight, excitement, and gratefulness to anxiety, fear, and insecurity. The rare combination of both joy and fear overwhelmed me because I knew, in just a few short hours, I would be married once again.*

After my divorce from Alyson, I swore I would never even consider dating again—let alone getting married. I'd been wounded so deeply, and I didn't think I could ever trust again. However, God had different plans for me. For some reason, He thought it would be fun to play this game with me called, "You won't be able to resist her." I thought I could easily win at this game because I didn't want to have anything to do with women for the rest of my life. I'd just accepted the fact that I was going to be a bachelor for the rest of my life, and honestly, a part of me was looking forward to the freedom of singleness. I could do all of my favorite hobbies whenever I wanted, travel wherever I wanted, dress however I wanted, and spend my money on whatever I wanted without consulting anyone. I liked my chances at winning this game, so I agreed to play. Then along came Carrie.

What I failed to take into consideration was the fact that God knows me better than I know myself. He knew exactly what kind of woman would capture my attention, and Carrie was that woman. In a way, God had rigged this game. But then again, He is God, and that is what He does. Not to mention, after I first laid eyes on her, I didn't even mind if He did rig the game—I just wanted to meet her.

Even though I was interested in Carrie, I didn't ask her out right away. Quite frankly, I was still in shock that I was even considering asking a woman on a date after I'd sworn them off for good. I also learned that she was in the process of obtaining her master's degree for clinical counseling and was taking care of her two girls, Chloe and Sarah, who were ages 7 and 5. Needless to say, her hands were full as a single mom, and I didn't want to take up even more of her time.

Besides, I wasn't exactly thrilled about reentering the dating scene even though I was interested in her. But all of that logic was thrown out the window after about six weeks of getting to know her. I finally got up the nerve to ask her out, and she said yes. Not only that, but after our first date, she made it clear that, in no uncertain terms, I was not allowed to date any other woman except her. I was never the sharpest tool in the shed when it came to women, but I was pretty sure she meant business, and I'd better not disappoint. So, that was the start of our two-year dating relationship.

Given that both Carrie and I came from previous marriages, neither of us wanted to risk another failed marriage. Throughout our dating relationship, we were very intentional about getting to know each other and worked hard to figure out if we were well-matched. For starters, we didn't follow the cultural approach to dating by moving in together as a test for compatibility. Instead, we made sure our beliefs and values were aligned. We wanted to make sure we were healed from our past marriages and weren't holding on to any form of bitterness. We also put a priority on knowing each other personally over simply doing activities together. We took our time progressing the relationship, and we slowly introduced our girls to one another. Our intentional dating relationship provided numerous opportunities to demonstrate that we were willing to take a sacrificial-giving approach to commitment. Most importantly, we consistently talked about our faith, prayed together regularly, and spent many hours trying to figure out how we might further God's kingdom as a couple if we decided to marry.

And today it was finally here—we were getting married. Everything seemed perfect, yet I was filled with fear. I couldn't find anything that caused concern or would prevent me from spending the rest of my life with her, but I was still scared to death to enter into a second marriage. What if I missed something? What if she changes after we're married? What if I change? What if we fail miserably in a stepfamily environment? All of these thoughts flooded my mind as I waited alone in my home, counting down the hours until I arrived at the church.

Once I arrived at the church and checked that everything was set up as planned, I began to settle into the events that were about to take place in just a couple hours. I was still nervous and scared, but the peace that transcends all understanding began to comfort me. If courage is defined as persistence in spite of fear, then getting married for the second time was the most courageous move I've ever made in my life. Once I saw Carrie walk down the aisle, all of my fears melted away. I knew she was the one, and I knew God had brought us together for a special purpose. I made a commitment to myself that very day—I would always pursue Carrie like Christ pursues me.

* * *

When anyone uses the term "blessed," the person implies God (or at a minimum a higher power or divine being) has provided something that brings a sense of happiness, joy, and/or fulfillment. In other words, a person has received something pleasant, and they either want others to know they've received something pleasant or desire to give credit to the One who has given them the something pleasant. In most cases, the person is showing a level of gratitude for the pleasure and enjoyment they've received.

Look up #Blessed on social media, and you'll find some common themes. Family and relationships appear to top the charts when it comes to making people feel blessed. This makes perfect sense because God designed mankind for relationships. Some of the deepest needs of a person are to feel accepted and included. Another common theme surrounds material blessings. People love to share the best versions of themselves on social media by posting pictures of their gorgeous families, tropical beach vacations, picture perfect homes, new job promotions, or career milestones. To be sure they don't appear too proud, included within their post is the humble statement, "I'm so blessed."

But is this what being blessed is all about?

What if I don't possess the things that others say they are blessed to have? Does that mean I'm not blessed?

Much of our misguided thinking about what it means to be blessed comes from a misunderstanding of the word "blessing." Most people define God's blessing as something that brings pleasure and enjoyment in the moment. These blessings typically are linked to positive emotions such as delight, thankfulness, connectedness, confidence, satisfaction, and empowerment.

I used to think that God's blessings came in the form of material blessings, so I rationalized that nothing was wrong with the next job promotion. I wasn't sinning against anyone by purchasing a bigger house, bigger TV, or luxury car. Nothing was wrong with ensuring my wife and daughter lived in an upscale and safe neighborhood. I loved them and wanted to give them the best I could provide, and I didn't see anything wrong with that.

After a period of time, I began to measure God's love for me by how much blessing I received. I assumed that as long as I was receiving that which I desired, then God's grace was shining upon me. I began to think that upward mobility was always God's plan for our family and never viewed the good and nice life as a curse. I completely missed the fact that bigger and better always meant that more time and attention had to be focused on obtaining the "blessings." The next promotion meant more time in the office. The bigger house meant more time keeping it clean and presentable for company. Private tennis lessons and competitive matches for Meredith meant more time finding and pursuing the best opportunities for advancing her athletic skills. Squeezing in family time for the three of us and extended family became challenging because of all our other commitments. Even vacations became difficult to schedule. Our calendars were maxed out, and we were exhausted from running non-stop. Our desire was to live the good and nice life, but it came with a cost. After we became accustomed to this hectic life, I continued to pursue what I thought was harmless and failed to realize that I'd begun pursuing God's blessings over God Himself.

WORSHIPING THE AMORAL

What the American Pharisee typically identifies as a "blessing" often becomes a barrier between the person and God. If the person is more focused on being blessed than being connected to God, the person is no longer worshiping God, but rather what one hopes to receive from God. This, again, is linked to the person's commitment to God. It is a needs-seeking type of commitment, where people are interested in God as long as they are getting what they want. In this scenario, no real commitment exists because it is conditional. It's also possible that the person started out with a legitimate, sacrificial giving type of commitment to God but, along the way, became distracted by ambition and the pleasures of life and began pursuing these over God Himself. Jesus warned about both of these scenarios when He gave the parable of the four soils:

Those on the rocky soil are those who when they hear, receive the word with joy; and these have no firm root; they believe for a while, and in time of temptation fall away. The seed which fell among the thorns, these are the ones who have heard, and as they go on their way they are choked with worries and riches and pleasures of this life, and bring no fruit to maturity. (Luke 8:13-14)

Clearly, Jesus warns that failing to have a real commitment to the Lord (the rocky soil) and letting the good life distract you from God (the thorny soil) are dangers we must all be aware of.

If Jesus were to visit self-proclaimed Christians across America, He would observe an army of American Pharisees who are excited about consuming whatever God has to give but aren't too interested in giving anything beyond what their busy schedule or affluent budget will allow. They spend more time worrying about saving in their 401k than about saving the lost. Their weekly budget for the coffee shop is greater than what they have set aside for giving to the poor. Parents spend more time transporting their children to school activities and travel sports than talking to them about God. Time spent on entertainment far exceeds the time spent building relationships and sharing faith with others.

So, are abundance, prosperity, and time spent enjoying life here on earth evil? This is an interesting question to consider, and one that should be reflected upon constantly. All good things come from God, and He has given to us generously. But as soon as we take something that God has given us and desire it above God or prefer it over Him, then we have taken something that is by nature amoral (neither good nor evil) and turned it into an idol. This idol that perhaps doesn't seem too harmful is actually incredibly vile and evil because we have forsaken God for something less than God. Things that God intended to be very good—marriage, sex, family, comfort, security, joy, serving others, and belonging—can become idols if we prefer those things over God Himself. Pursuing God's blessings over Him is quite arguably the greatest tragedy a person could ever experience. Thus, God's warning to His people thousands of years ago is the same warning we must heed today lest we fall into this trap: "Your heart will become proud, and you will forget the Lord your God" (Deuteronomy 8:14).

When I look back on my life as an American Pharisee, I saw things as fairly black and white. I prided myself in having this type of clarity but failed to realize my supposed clarity was actually blinding me. I generally viewed pleasant events as blessings and unpleasant events as curses. Here are just a few of the big items in my life and how I viewed them:

Pleasant Events ("blessings")

- Losing weight
- Graduating from college
- Marriage / Family
- Career advancement
- Living in an upscale neighborhood
- Leisure time / Entertainment

Unpleasant Events ("curses")

- Being teased and ridiculed for being obese
- Chronic back pain
- Dropping out of law school
- Betrayal
- Divorce
- Letting go of the "American Dream"

As any rational person would conclude, I desired pleasant events and detested the unpleasant. Most of my adult life, I pursued the pleasant and wanted God to bless me with them. As I received from God, I continued to pursue Him, but in reality, I was just chasing after that which "blessed" me. What I really wanted was an enjoyable life here on earth.

TRUE DEFINITION OF BLESSING

Pleasant events or circumstances cannot be the litmus test for determining whether a person is blessed. Just because I like something doesn't mean it's good for me. Take food for example. I like pizza, ice cream, bacon, and tortilla chips, but I know I can't sustain a diet with these foods and expect to be healthy. Likewise, I like happiness, but too much of it will cause me to miss out on true joy and contentment. I like comfort, but too much of it will prevent me from taking active steps of faith. I like success, but too much of it will cause me to rely on my own abilities instead of God's.

If I believe God is good and has made me in the image of His likeness, then anything that draws me closer to

Him is a blessing and anything that draws me further away from God becomes a curse. Understanding this truth has completely transformed how I view what it means to be blessed. God can take the ugly, the tragic, and turn them into a blessing—that which draws us closer to Him. Thus, blessing is no longer defined in simple terms of good or bad, fun or unpleasant, but it's now defined in its intended sense: true blessing is closeness with God.

> IF I BELIEVE GOD IS GOOD AND HAS MADE ME IN THE IMAGE OF HIS LIKENESS, THEN ANYTHING THAT DRAWS ME CLOSER TO HIM IS A BLESSING AND ANYTHING THAT DRAWS ME FURTHER AWAY FROM GOD BECOMES A CURSE.

We can now recognize that God will use *all* things for good to those who love Him and are called according to His purpose. Nothing is beyond God's capability. When reflecting on the major unpleasant events in my life, I can honestly call them blessings because every single unpleasant event ultimately drew me closer to God.

American Pharisees and most skeptics tend to view this definition of blessing as merely taking a bad situation and trying to find something good in it. Apart from God, their assessment is accurate. However, declaring an unpleasant event a blessing from God is quite different for those who believe. We are not taking something bad and rationalizing it into something good. We are acknowledging and accepting the fact that something bad *has* happened, but in the midst of our sorrow and hurt, we draw near to God. We don't ignore the fact that we want the pain removed, and we may even beg God to eliminate the pain. But we never lose sight of the fact that our most important need is our connection with God. If our primary motive for drawing near to Him is for "pain elimination," then our drawing near to Him becomes self-serving, and we miss the true blessing of being in His presence while we navigate the grieving process.

Many times, we become so focused on pain avoidance and eliminating it altogether that we miss the opportunity of relationally knowing God in the midst of our trial. Nothing is wrong with casting our cares upon the Lord; He genuinely wants us to bring our trials to Him (Philippians 4:6-7, I Peter 5:6-7). But when we prefer the removal of the trial over our relational connection with God Himself, then what we are actually saying is, "My happiness and wellbeing are more important to me than God." In essence, we are treating God like a genie, as we attempt to lord our will over His will and fail to treat Him as Lord. As we go through trials, make God our primary focus, and we will experience God in a real way as we endure the trials. As the psalmist says, "My flesh and my heart may fail, But God is the strength of my heart and my portion forever" (Psalms 73:26).

SMASHING IDOLS

Nothing is wrong with asking God to bless our lives, but we can't lose sight of the truth that Christ has asked us to lay down our lives (Matt. 16:25). Similar to how unpleasant events have drawn me closer to God, I also recognize how some very pleasurable moments prevented me from laying down my life for the sake of Christ. I was so focused on receiving the "good" that I stopped pursuing the One who is good.

The pursuit of the American Dream is appealing, and the former Pharisee Paul had something to say about the dangers of wanting to be rich:

Those who want to get rich fall into temptation and a snare and many foolish and harmful desires which plunge men into ruin and destruction. For the love of money is a root of all sorts of evil, and some by longing for it have wandered away from the faith and pierced themselves with many griefs. (I Timothy 6:9-10)

In my days as an American Pharisee, I knew this verse well, but I always discounted what Paul was saying because I convinced myself that I didn't love money—I just wanted to have enough so I could live a comfortable life and not have to worry about where my next paycheck was coming from. I also took seriously the warning that some have even wandered away from the faith, but I convinced myself that I was an exception to the "some." As long as I continued to give God credit for my success and gave 10% of my income, I didn't see how I could possibly fall into the trap of wandering away from the faith. After all, why would I walk away from the God who was blessing me with affluence? But my heart was becoming proud with prosperity, and I began forgetting the Lord my God.

THE BLESSING OF SUFFERING

It wasn't until God healed me emotionally from the divorce and healed me physically from my embolism that I began to realize I'd completely misunderstood what blessing meant. God used these tragic events to reveal to me that I was pursuing His blessings over Him. The Lord convicted my heart that I was worshiping the American Trinity of happiness, comfort, and success, and this realization resulted in some radical changes to my life.

When we envision the love of God, we have a tendency to only think about the happy side of His love, such as His compassion, kindness, gentleness, mercy, and grace. We easily forget that He will do *whatever it takes* for us to see His love. This means He will allow us to become broken if that's what is required for us to turn back to Him. Words cannot express my gratitude towards God's perfect love that broke me down and hurt me deeply. It is not that God desired for me to suffer a divorce. That would mean God desires His children to suffer the consequences of sin, and we know from scripture that true love is not malevolent. However, God, in His sovereignty, will use the negative effects of sin to draw us closer to Him. This is an awesome testimony to His divine redemptive power, absolute authority, unceasing grace, and perfect love for us. Because of His love for me, He took the sin of divorce and used it to reveal to me a much deeper and more pervasive problem—my own self-righteousness and pre-conceived idea of what it meant to be a Christian.

One doesn't have to search far to see that life doesn't always turn out okay for God's chosen ones. Jacob's son Joseph was sold into slavery and falsely accused of committing adultery. David had to live on the run because King Saul wanted to kill him. After producing a miracle at Mount Carmel, Elijah feared for his life as King Ahab and Jezebel wanted to kill him. And who can forget Job? This man went through terrible suffering. In a short matter of time, he lost all of his livestock, servants, his children, and contracted sores all over his body.

Things don't get much better in the New Testament either. John the Baptist was beheaded for telling the truth. All of the disciples experienced persecution, were beaten, or experienced violent deaths. Jesus Himself was falsely accused of blasphemy and put to death, even though He was completely innocent. Every hero of the Bible went through some form of suffering for the sake of carrying God's message.

One of the statements that disturbs me the most in the Bible occurs when Jesus appears to Ananias and instructs him to go to Saul, give Saul his sight back, and anoint him with the Holy Spirit. When Ananias hesitates because of Saul's persecution of the Christians, Jesus replies, "Go, for he is a chosen instrument of Mine, to bear My name before the Gentiles and kings and the sons of Israel; **for I will show him how much he must suffer for My name's sake**." Wait a second—Jesus would allow His chosen people to suffer? Yes.

God brought me to the very edge of where my faith stopped to reveal that I was committing idolatry by pursuing His blessings instead of pursuing Him. In His holy mercifulness, God gave me another chance to turn away from my sin of being an American Pharisee and turn back to Him. I responded to this opportunity by giving up my idols of happiness, comfort, and success. I smashed the idol of happiness by allowing myself to embrace suffering instead of trying to avoid it. I smashed the idol of comfort by intentionally taking bold steps of faith that made me uncomfortable. I smashed the idol of success by departing from the world's definition and embracing real success by pursuing God and passing along the goodness and grace He has given me to others.

Going through the process of suffering was very painful, and giving up my idols was also very unpleasant. Taking up my cross, denying myself daily, and handing control over to Christ was absolutely frightening. Yet, I wouldn't trade any of this for all of the happiness, comfort, and success this world has to offer. By drawing near to God in the midst of my suffering, He drew close to me. By smashing my idols, I saw Him more clearly. God healed me as I pursued Him, and this healing allowed me to love Carrie like Christ loves the church.

SUCCESSFUL MARRIAGES ENDURE SUFFERING

Most people incorrectly believe the goal in marriage is to have a happy, fun marriage. Without a doubt, healthy marriages are filled with happy and fun moments, but amusement isn't the end goal in life nor is it the end goal of marriage. Christ-honoring marriages must be eternally focused and not earth focused. Life on earth is too short not to be eternally minded.

Newlyweds become quickly disappointed when they discover that marriage isn't always fun. In actuality, marriage is a lot of work, and it requires spouses to endure suffering. But just like our relationship with Christ, the pain and discomfort from being stretched causes us to grow, and that in turn allows our marriages to grow and become stronger.

The reality is that marriage is not a fairy tale that ends in happily ever after. What defines a successful marriage is not the absence of conflict or suffering, but rather how the two will come together in the midst of conflict. Successful marriages will endure planned suffering, consequential suffering, and tragic suffering. In these moments, spouses of healthy marriages will build up, encourage, and comfort each other. Apologizing, asking for

> WHAT DEFINES A SUCCESSFUL MARRIAGE IS NOT THE ABSENCE OF CONFLICT OR SUFFERING, BUT RATHER HOW THE TWO WILL COME TOGETHER IN THE MIDST OF CONFLICT.

forgiveness, and offering forgiveness become sacrifices of humility and surrender. Prioritizing the pursuit of God over pursuing each other teaches spouses how to love their spouse with more compassion, kindness, gentleness, grace, and mercy as they learn from God's example.

BLESSED DISCOMFORT

Pursuing God will make us uncomfortable. The idea of taking up our cross every day to follow Christ from a human perspective is not only humiliating, it is painful. It is humiliating because the world laughs at us. We are forced to make decisions that go against the cultural norm, and people will ridicule us. Taking up our crosses daily is painful because following Him takes priority over EVERYTHING—our dreams, desires, pursuits, goals, relationships, feelings, ideals…EVERYTHING. No matter how noble and righteous our intentions might be, if we elevate *anything* above our relationship with Jesus, we are committing idolatry. To lose everything so that we might be saved is a very costly proposition from the world's view. Yet, if we have indeed lost our lives for the sake of Christ, then we are acting in faith that God will offer us something better than anything we can obtain here on earth. If we commit our lives to Jesus by choosing to take on His name, His identity, His message, then we can be assured we will suffer for His name's sake. However, God has promised that all of this suffering is nothing compared to the glory that will be revealed to us in eternity. Our reward far outweighs the pain and struggle of making Him known to the world, so we endure planned suffering.

Likewise, growing in a marriage is also uncomfortable. Two imperfect people come together as one, so conflict will be sure to arise. Just as we surrender ourselves to Christ in humility, spouses surrender their personal self-interests for the sake of strengthening the relationship. Throughout the life of the marriage, the relationship will grow as each pursues Christ and reflects His love towards the other. I failed to recognize this truth in my marriage with Alyson, but God completely redeemed that which was broken and turned it into something beautiful with Carrie. While I am blessed beyond all measure to have her as my wife, I do not lose sight that God is the source of this blessing. He has once again entrusted me with the gift of marriage, and I will forever love and pursue Carrie as Christ pursues the Church.

* * *

Questions for Reflection:

1. Take a moment to consider why you chose to follow Christ. Did you choose a conditional needs-seeking type of commitment because of what you thought He could provide you? Did you choose an unconditional sacrificial-giving commitment of humility, surrender, and obedience because He is God?

2. Are you currently pursuing God over God's blessings? What evidence can you give to support your answer?

3. How does understanding the true definition of blessing change your perspective on the terrible moments in your life?

4. When hardship comes into your marriage, how might you begin fighting for your relationship

instead of fighting for your rights? If you are single, what should you look for in your future spouse that will indicate he/she is willing to put your relationship above personal preferences?

12

WALKING IN FAITH: THE GREATEST JOURNEY

"Faith comes by hearing and hearing by the word of Christ"
Romans 10:17

"Whatever does not proceed from faith is sin."
Romans 14:23

"And without faith it is impossible to please Him."
Hebrews 11:6

JULY 2018

*I*t'd been four years, almost to the exact day, since I'd sat along the bank at Alum Creek and questioned why God was giving me a second chance in life. And it was almost eight years to the day of when I'd sat in my kayak and questioned whether or not I even believed in God. Now here I was, standing face to face with two critical steps of faith—walking away from the corporate world altogether in order to invest more time in kingdom building work and selling the home I'd once considered the pinnacle of my success.

My career in the financial industry was the only job I was really familiar with. I had dedicated over twenty-two years to climbing the corporate ladder, and looking back, I recognized that I'd invested more hours into my career than into anything else throughout my entire life. This reality really bothered me, particularly over the last four years. Actually, it was kind of depressing. Exceeding client expectations, meeting corporate goals, and increasing shareholder value might be highly valued in the corporate world, but all of this has very little value in the context of eternity. Yet, I had dedicated the majority of my life to such meaningless activity. In the corporate world, the almighty dollar is worshipped and will ultimately win every business decision because corporations are manmade institutions with the sole goal of providing a financial return to its investors. Senior corporate executives will say their company exists to provide some sort of benefit to its customers; they'll claim that clients come first and that employees are their most valued asset. However, the reality is that corporations must answer to their investors, and the dollar always triumphs over having the best product, client satisfaction, and loyalty to employees. Successful corporations will never value their employees above the expected cost to produce its goods or services. This is basic economics, and it makes logical sense. But it's based on man's economy, not God's.

Throughout my career, I always tried to value people above products and budgets. I also had a few good role models throughout my career, such as Anne who took a genuine interest in others. Unfortunately, we were the exception to the rule. Most managers, particularly in senior and executive management, are concerned with only one thing—their own agendas. Their words may say they are committed to their employees, but they have a needs-seeking conditional type of commitment that is founded upon their own success. Their true sacrificial commitment is to their own promotions and personal wealth. It is nothing more than an adult game of king of the hill, where people are constantly trying to climb the corporate ladder while others are constantly trying to knock them down. The further up the ladder they go, the more aggressive and intense the game becomes. While career advancement is highly valued in corporate America, it has very little worth in God's Kingdom.

The Lord had been revealing these truths to me over the last eight years, and my heart became convicted—I no longer desired to work for a big corporation. After my embolism, I saw life from a very different perspective. My true desire was to be transformed into the image of His likeness and to be actively involved with His Kingdom work. I began to see that God was calling me to break free from the prison of the corporate world, but I didn't know what my next career would be. All I knew was that I needed to take a step of faith into the unknown and trust that God would take care of my family and me. To most unbelievers, and many believers, deciding to leave a successful career with nothing substantial lined up does not appear logical or wise. But I'm now convinced that it's wiser to obey God's calling than to rely on my own logic or understanding.

Carrie and I had been praying together for a few years for clarity on when was the right time for me to leave, and that opportunity first began to appear in January of 2018. We both sensed that I needed to focus on my writing and become certified as a Christian life coach. Knowing this type of career change could not sustain the kind of living we were familiar with; we began the process of downsizing.

The first significant move was selling our home, and this was particularly difficult for me. The home we currently lived in was the home I had built back in 2007 at the height of my pursuit of the American Dream. The home had a lot of sentimental value because it represented my achievements.

It was also the house that provided a sanctuary when I came home from a stressful day's work. It provided a place of healing for me after the divorce as I spent numerous hours in it praying, reflecting, and growing in God's Word. It was where Meredith and I experienced a new beginning with Carrie and the girls. Life happened in this house, and while I knew it wasn't the house that provided the life, it was familiar, dependable, and where memories were made. However, I knew that God was leading me in a different direction, and leaving this home was part of that plan. I knew I had to give it up even if it was going to be painful.

So, there we were. Almost eight years to the exact date of my questioning God's existence. I left my career, and we sold our home. We moved into a home almost half the size of our old one, and I began my career as a life coach. Carrie and I didn't make these significant decisions because it was fun and entertaining. We made these sacrifices purely out of love for God. Our desire is to grow in our connection with Him, and we know that growth in relationships requires selfless sacrifice. The amazing part in all of this is that the pain, discomfort, and fear of stepping out into the unknown has continuously been met with a growing connection with Christ and each other, and those connections far outweigh any joy this world could ever provide. We have learned through experience that suffering does, in fact, precede glory, and the sacrifices we have made now seem trivial when compared to experiencing God's activity in our lives as we continue to glorify Him. This is just one small example of what it looks like to walk in the faith that saves us.

* * *

As Scripture reveals, the evidence of our faith can be seen in the fruit that we bear. A branch is incapable of producing fruit, as only the vine can produce the fruit. The job of the branches is to abide in the vine, and the vine does its work of producing the fruit through each branch. As Christians, we are the branches and Christ is the vine. We cannot abide in Christ while also following our own agendas, regardless of how virtuous, noble, and righteous we think our plans might be. Our human view of morality is defined as simply doing our best to obey God's law, but real obedience means that my total identity is in Christ and I put my entire trust in Him. By resting in Christ's identity and living out the faith that has saved me, I abide in Him and begin bearing fruit—the good works He created for me to walk in before time began. Sadly, I wasn't fruitful throughout much of my life as a Christ follower.

For many years, I confused being fruitful with being productive. I thought that as long as I kept myself busy with serving, then I was being fruitful. But in reality, I was just keeping myself busy. Don't get me wrong; I was a tremendous help to my church and community, but I wasn't bearing any fruit. What I mean by this is that I was doing all of these activities out of my own sense of duty, responsibility, and obligation. I never really prayed about whether or not I should volunteer for a particular position or activity at church. I just observed a need and filled it or said yes when someone asked me to help. I was being obedient for obedience's sake, but I wasn't being obedient for Christ's sake. I wasn't asking *Him* where *He* wanted me to serve. I just used my own judgment to determine if the need was worth meeting and whether or not I wanted to do it. While I may have been expressing obedience, I wasn't expressing much faith.

American Pharisees are experts at falsifying evidence of their faith. They gravitate towards good deeds and claim they are producing the fruit of the Spirit. They say they trust God, but they aren't willing to let go of their own ambitions to follow Him. They say they are blessed, but what they claim is a blessing actually distances them from God. For example, I measured my faith by how much work I was doing instead of examining my commitment and connectedness to Christ. It was much easier to measure faith in terms of good deeds because they are tangible. It's a lot harder to measure faith by how much we are relying on God to guide our every step. I misled myself into thinking that I was bearing fruit and completely missed the fact that I can't produce fruit unless I allow Christ to work in me.

To avoid falling into this trap of falsifying evidence of my faith, I now often reflect on the following questions:

- Do I see evidence of God's transformational work within me?

- Do I look forward to investing more of my time, money, abilities, and efforts into eternal treasures rather than into worldly treasures?

- Do I desire God's agenda and actively pursue it over my own personal agenda?

- Do I act upon God's truth even when I do not know the outcome?

- Do I act upon God's truth even when I know the outcome will be uncomfortable or unpleasant?

- Do I desire to share my experience of growing closer to God with others?

- Do I desire for others to come into a saving faith relationship with God?

If I answer "no" to any of these questions or answer "yes" while not actively experiencing them in my daily life, then I admit to God that I'm falsifying evidence of my faith and need Him to show me where I'm veering off track. This isn't just a one-time prayer where I then go on living my life the best I know how. This is something I will continue to search for until God reveals it to me. I know the root issue is with me and not God, so I search until He reveals it to me because I don't want any barriers in our relationship.

BUT EVEN IF...

Taking steps of faith can be scary because we are relying on something other than our five senses to make a decision. In fact, Tony Evans has stated that if we rely solely on our five senses, then we are not walking in faith.[10] We might be expressing obedience, but we are not acting in faith. Taking true steps of faith mean we will not know the outcome or only have a general understanding of what the outcome *could* be. Thus, true steps of faith will always possess a "but even if" component. All of our big decisions should be rooted in Scripture, prayer, affirmation from other believers, and an understanding of current circumstances. But even when we incorporate these four factors into our decision-making process, we may not know exactly which option we should take or the outcome of a tough decision. In Scripture, the book of Daniel clearly illustrates the "but even if" component of walking in faith through the lives of Shadrach, Meshach, and Abednego, three believers who were most likely going to be put to death by the king for their faith:

Shadrach, Meshach and Abednego replied to the king, "O Nebuchadnezzar, we do not need to give you an answer concerning this matter. If it be so, our God whom we serve is able to deliver us from the furnace of blazing fire; and He will deliver us out of your hand, O king. ***But even if*** He does not, let it be known to you, O king, that we are not going to serve your gods or worship the golden image that you have set up." (Daniel 3:16-18)

Shadrach, Meshach and Abednego were put to a serious test of faith. They knew that God could deliver them out of the hand of King Nebuchadnezzar through a divine miracle, and they also knew that, because of their faith, they might be incinerated in the furnace. Their reply to the king reveals much about their faith: (1) they acknowledged the truth of God's power to do the miraculous and (2) they also acknowledged the truth that God was not *required* to deliver them because they were faithful to Him. Their reply actually contains the "but even if" component of walking in faith—they were not going to compromise their faith in God even if He did not deliver them.

I love this particular Scripture because it captures the essence of how we are to walk in faith. There are a couple key phrases that we can pull from their reply and use them to fill in the blanks with our own particular faith challenges. The result becomes the framework by which we are to walk in faith.

If it be so, our God will _____ _____ (fill in the blank).

But even if He does not, _____ _____ (fill in what will not be compromised).

Remember, there are no guarantees in using this formula to create a faith statement. If you use this framework, there is no guarantee God will do what He is capable of doing. The faith building power in this statement comes from what you believe about the statement in your heart. Do you believe the statement to be true regardless of the outcome, or are you more interested in a favorable result? If you can answer that question with all sincerity and honesty, then you will have a pretty good idea if you are walking in authentic faith or trying to use God for your own purposes.

WHEN FAITH INTERSECTS WITH SUFFERING

American Pharisees tend to believe they should somehow be exempt from suffering. They believe that upon becoming a Christian their lives will be void of any suffering or that diligently obeying God's laws will keep them in God's good favor. This view is simply not Biblical. Jesus tells us very clearly that in this world we will suffer (John 16:33). He also says that believers will not experience any special favor over non-believers (Matt. 5:45). Until our broken world is fully restored by God in His perfect timing, no one will be exempt from suffering.

Even though every person will experience suffering at some point, those who proclaim a saving faith in Christ are actually called to suffer for Christ. One truth that exists throughout the Bible is that faith and suffering are closely linked together. In fact, they are almost inseparable. As much as I tried to avoid this truth in my American Pharisee days, I've now come to realize that suffering is not just a part of life in this broken world—it is a way of life for those who are really committed to following

Christ. I admit that I still struggle with this reality and don't like the thought of suffering. However, I continue choosing to give up what the world values in exchange for a growing and thriving relationship with Christ. And as a result of my sacrificial commitment to follow Him, I have experienced many blessings that far outweighs any suffering that I have endured.

Jesus understood suffering. Before He went to the cross, He was fully aware of the suffering to come, and the reality of it led Him to sweat blood. This all happened in the Garden of Gethsemane shortly before Judas betrayed Him. Jesus knew He must die so that we could be redeemed, yet He was so distressed about this reality that, along with sweating blood, He pleaded with the Father to take away His suffering. But, as we know, He ultimately surrendered to His Father's will when He prayed, "Father, if You are willing, remove this cup from Me; yet not My will, but Yours be done" (Luke 22:42). Jesus' prayer provides for us a perfect example of what to pray in the midst of our own suffering. His prayer acknowledges the Father's sovereignty over suffering while, at the same time, shows Jesus' willingness to surrender to the Father's authority. Thus, Jesus willingly suffered as part of His perfect plan of redemption, even though it was something that He did not desire to endure.

Jesus' suffering was more than the agony of being crucified. As Scripture reveals, shortly after asking the Father to put a halt on His crucifixion, Jesus, nevertheless, finds Himself hanging on the cross. In the midst of His pain, He cried out, "My God, My God, why have You forsaken me?" (Matthew 27:46). Clearly, the physical pain of the crucifixion was unbearable, but there's even more—the pain of carrying the sins of the world compounded by the pain of separation from the Father is something our human minds cannot even comprehend.

Imagine for a moment the pain and sorrow resulting from a sin you committed or a sin that was committed against you. Jesus didn't just carry the pain and sorrow of that one sin, He freely gave His life for the sins of the world—going all the way back to the beginning of time and extending into the unknown future. Not only did Jesus, the Son of Man, have to bear the pain of all those sins on the cross, He also had to experience separation from the Father while bearing these sins. Even though the separation would be temporary, Jesus experienced the pain of separation from the Father when Jesus needed Him the most.

Because of what He had to endure, it's no wonder that Jesus begged the Father to change His circumstances despite knowing His purpose for coming to earth. Yet Jesus remained obedient. He knew that conditional obedience was just another term for disobedience. He preferred glorifying the Father and saving mankind over the suffering He had to endure—it was an expression of true love for the Father, for you, and for me.

Jesus knows what it means to suffer. As a matter of fact, He's known the greatest suffering because He experienced the greatest injustice: paying the penalty for sins He didn't commit. But He surrendered Himself in humility, knowing, in the end, that the Father would be glorified and Christ would be glorified in Him. His suffering was planned before time began because He pre-determined that we were worth suffering for.

Defeating the Enemy

The enemy will use our own tragic suffering as a weapon to create doubt in our hearts. However, God will use our tragedies as opportunities to reveal Himself to us and to grow us into the image of His likeness. But here is the key—we must allow Him to do so by trusting Him in the midst of our pain.

We may never get the answer to the question, "Why am I suffering?" Even if we do get the answer, it will not be sufficient to take away the pain. But this is where faith comes alive. When we believe God's Word to be true despite our circumstances, we take a step beyond the end of ourselves (our own knowledge, ability, effort) and step into the unknown and unfamiliar—a step of faith.

When we take a step of faith, our faith begins to grow because we must accept God's truth without any evidence that a greater purpose will result from the tragedy. As Scripture tells us, when we suffer for God, it does not go unnoticed: "For what credit is there if, when you sin and are harshly treated, you endure it with patience? But if when you do what is right and suffer for it you patiently endure it, this finds favor with God" (I Peter 2:20). What Peter is saying is we should expect consequential suffering for doing wrong, but if we endure unjust suffering patiently, then we will find favor with God. By responding to suffering with steps of faith, we stop second-guessing God and begin trusting Him in spite of our circumstances.

Through suffering, I have come to learn that God, in His amazing love, allowed me to endure great pain, so that I could have a closer relationship with Him. I can clearly see that He did not cause the divorce, and the divorce was never intended to be His expressive will since marriage between a man and a woman is a reflection of Christ's relationship with the Church (Ephesians 5:31-32). God is never responsible for any broken marriage or bad relationship. Human sin caused my divorce—not God. Sin is the culprit for everything that does not align to God's character and original design. But in His amazing freedom, He permits sin and brokenness to exist, so mankind may possess a free will. In the end, it was His *permissive* will that *allowed* the divorce to occur.

But God doesn't just *allow* sin to occur without a purpose. His mighty sovereignty and providence reign above all of the sin and brokenness in this world. He has redeemed, He is redeeming, and He will redeem all of the negative effects of sin in His perfect time. This is the God who created us, and this is the God we have the privilege of worshiping.

DEALING WITH DOUBT

How should we deal with suffering that causes us to doubt our faith? Embrace the pain, turn to God, pour your heart out to Him, confess the doubt, and ask Him to help you to trust Him. I don't want to underestimate just how difficult this is, because I know firsthand. I struggled for many months after that day at Clearfork Reservoir, and to be honest, there were times when I thought God had completely abandoned me. I couldn't sense His presence, His comfort, His peace, or any hope whatsoever. Many evenings, I read the Bible trying to find answers, but none could satisfy my hurting heart. I vividly remember pouring my heart out to God praying, "God, You feel absent from this situation, and I can't make any sense out of why You would allow this to happen. You hate divorce, but You are allowing it to happen in my life? Even though it goes against everything within me, I'm going to believe You have not forsaken me even though my circumstances, emotions, intellect, and logic say otherwise."

I must confess that I hated going through this process—putting my faith in God when everything else around me appeared to be contradicting His Word. I hated that I was angry at God. Most of all, I hated the pain that came from suffering. My heart was torn, and there was nothing I could do to mend it. But I figured since I'd spent the majority of my life following Jesus, I was going to take Him at His word. At the time, I didn't realize it, but I was acting in faith. I was choosing to believe God irrespective of my circumstances.

Even though I doubted and was unsure about many things, I chose to trust Him. Sometimes people can falsely believe that faith must be exercised without *any* doubt. But if we are going to be moved beyond the end of ourselves, then we naturally will have doubts. Many of the great heroes of the Bible doubted at one time or another, yet what separated them from the faithless was that they chose to take the step of faith in spite of their doubts. Bold steps of faith might cause us to doubt the outcome, but they should never cause us to doubt God's character or abilities.

THE GREATEST BLESSING

Will God put an end to the evil that is present in this broken world? Yes. But it will be on His timetable, not ours. Just because events do not occur within our accepted timeframe, it does not mean they won't occur. God promises that a new day is coming, and He is faithful to His Word. The redemption of mankind and the end of suffering can be expressed in these three words: "It is finished." Through Christ Jesus, our Eternal Father has redeemed, is redeeming, and will redeem all of the brokenness that sin has created, is creating, and will create. And God will use something ugly, such as suffering, as the means to bring about His Kingdom. A.W. Tozer states it this way: "It is doubtful whether God will bless a man greatly until He has hurt him deeply."[11] This is a sobering reminder that God will allow suffering to rest upon His children as part of His overall plan for redeeming the world. Only God can take something ugly and turn it into something that ultimately glorifies Him. As His children, we are eternally healed from the pain and suffering this world has delivered, is delivering, and will deliver to us. If we have not yet experienced this healing, it is only a matter of time before we experience it. This is His promise to us—through all of our suffering, redemption, and healing, God will be glorified; thus, He fulfills the end goal of the Gospel.

THE PARADOX OF SUFFERING

Here is what I find bizarre: I never want to go through something as painful as divorce again, yet I would never trade that horrible experience for anything. My suffering ultimately drew me closer to God, and that alone is a blessing greater than I could have ever imagined. It's amazing how going through a crisis can draw a person closer to God. It's even more amazing how God can know exactly what we need even if it's something we don't want. This is a powerful testimony to God's divine providence that is so easily overlooked in the midst of suffering. We must cling to God's answer to suffering: He causes all things to work together for the good of those who love Him and are called according to His purpose. God will one day eliminate all suffering, but until the world is fully restored, He has provided an answer to suffering—Himself.

For me, I needed to be set free from my distorted view of what it meant to be a Christian, and God used the divorce to ultimately achieve His good. Through this experience, I have learned that the American culture played a major role in distorting my view of God and faith in God. I didn't realize how distorted my beliefs were while I was suffering the divorce. Honestly, it took me years to understand the purpose of my pain. After a lot of prayer and reflection, I now know, without a doubt, I had to go through this period of brokenness. God hurt me deeply, so I could see Him more clearly. Pain was the means that forced me out of the American Pharisee religion. When we come to the end of ourselves, we are able to take a step of faith towards God. In doing so, we know Him more intimately and experience Him more fully.

> MY SUFFERING ULTIMATELY DREW ME CLOSER TO GOD, AND THAT ALONE IS A BLESSING GREATER THAN I COULD HAVE EVER IMAGINED.

Has suffering caused you to drift from God? Has planned suffering caused you to become more dependent on yourself and less dependent on God? Are you still feeling the painful effects of consequential suffering? Has tragedy gripped you to the point you are questioning God's goodness? Hope rests in these promises: "The Lord will not abandon His people, nor will He forsake His inheritance" (Psalms 94:14) and "He will wipe away every tear from their eyes; and there will no longer be any death; there will no longer be any mourning, or crying, or pain" (Revelation 21:4).

Since we are bound by time and are unable to know the future, the time when our tears will be wiped away remains a mystery, but we can trust His Word to be true. Hold on to the hope that you will be comforted, even when everything in you says otherwise. If you are currently in the pit of suffering and find yourself asking, "Why," turn to Him. Pour your heart out and weep. Tell Him how badly you hurt, how mad you are about it, and how you want the pain to go away. If we are children of God, we can be assured of this truth: "The righteous cry, and the Lord hears and delivers them out of all their troubles. The Lord is near to the broken hearted and saves those who are crushed in spirit" (Psalms 34:17-18).

He will heal.

He will restore.

He will deliver.

And He will do this in His perfect timing as He continues to restore the world that we messed up.

Why? Because He is God and He is faithful to His Word.

* * *

Questions for Reflection:

1. Where do you sense that God is encouraging you to take a step of faith that goes beyond your five senses? What doubt is preventing you from taking this step of faith? Is this doubt based on a personal fear or a distorted belief about God?

2. In terms of personal suffering, what circumstances or experiences have caused you to doubt what you know to be true about God's character and ability? Where is this doubt coming from? In what ways has this doubt hindered your relationship with God?

3. What are some active steps of faith that you can take to begin trusting God again, even if it goes against what you are feeling inside?

ACKNOWLEDGEMENTS

I am so grateful for my wife, Carrie, who not only encouraged me every step of the way, but she has also been fully supportive of my faith walk. Carrie, you mean the world to me, and I'm so thankful the Lord bridged the broken road that brought us together. There is no one else I would rather do life with than you.

Mom and Dad, thank you so much for raising me in a home environment that made Christ a priority and the foundation on which we live. The values you taught me as a child have played such an integral role in who I am today.

I want to thank Allison Myers for taking my manuscript and making me sound like an actual author. Your editing skills are amazing! Amy Moon, I want to thank you for proofreading my book and for providing so much valuable feedback. Thad Mertz, thanks for all of your feedback and suggestions. You are a life-long friend who has always challenged me in my faith. Our countless hours of pondering spiritual matters has been influential for sure. Meredith, thanks for helping me brainstorm ideas for my cover—you are so creative and artistic! Alfie, your finished cover design was simply a work of art, and I truly enjoyed working with you.

Troy Palermo, you are an incredible man of God. I have learned so much from you and I value our friendship. Bob Egolf and Scott Hawk, you guys have been pillars in my faith walk. I treasure our Friday morning discussions on life and building each other up in Christ. Thanks for keeping me accountable and for helping me grow in the faith. Special thanks to Dean Fulks and the entire Lifepoint Church staff for creating and maintaining such a wonderful place where people can come together to draw life from Christ and point others to Him.

Finally, and most importantly, I give all the credit for writing this book to The One who I was writing to—my Savior and Lord Jesus. Why He created a desire in me to write and chose me to convey a message of redemption and hope I may never know. And I don't have to know; I just have to trust Him who has given me this wonderful gift and remain faithful to Him in obedience. Jesus, this story is my love letter to You. Thank You for Your amazing grace of which I am so undeserving.

NOTES

1   John Piper. "A Beginner's Guide to 'Free Will.'" Desiring God. July 26, 2016. https://www. desiringgod.org

2   Charles Spurgeon. AZ Quotes. Accessed March 23, 2017. https://www.azquotes.com/quote/823773

3   Charles Spurgeon. *All of Grace.* 2013.

4   David Platt. *Radical: Taking Back Your Faith From The American Dream.* May 2010.

5   John Piper. "Sin Will Never Make You Happy." Desiring God. November 26, 2016. https://www. desiringgod.org

6   Adrian Rogers. "Cardboard Christians." LoveWorthFinding. April 22, 2011. https://www. lwf.org

7   James MacDonald. "Root Cause." March 2016. https://jamesmacdonald.com

8   Dean Fulks. Sermon presented at Lifepoint Church, Lewis Center, Ohio, October 2017.

9   "Am I Rich?" Remember the Poor. Accessed July 2016. https://irememberthepoor.org/3-2/

10   Tony Evans. "Concept of Faith." Tony Evans: The Urban Alternative. March 6, 2018. https://tonyevans.org

11   Aiden Wilson Tozer. *The Root of the Righteous.* 1955.

Kevin wants to hear from you. Connect with him at:
kevinhover.com

Coming Soon: American Pharisee study guide
for small groups.

CPSIA information can be obtained
at www.ICGtesting.com
Printed in the USA
LVHW080759281019
635534LV00003B/152/P